SURVIVAL SKILLS:

SURVIVE THE COMING FINANCIAL CRASH SIMPLY, SAFELY, AND CHEAPLY

Brian Stevens

All Rights Reserved

TABLE OF CONTENTS

INTRODUCTION 6

1 - SURVIVAL FOOD 10

    THE CANNED AND DRIED FOOD STORAGE PLAN 12

    OUR PERSONAL STORAGE PLAN 16

    CANNED-AND-DRIED FOOD RECIPES 19

    EAT WHAT YOU LIKE 33

    SHELF LIFE 35

    STORAGE CHECKLIST 42

    FREQUENTLY ASKED QUESTIONS 43

    RECOMMENDED RESOURCES 51

2 - WATER 53

    WATER TREATMENT GUDE 55

    ALTERNATE WATER SOURCES INSIDE YOUR HOME ... 58

    ALTERNATE WATER SOURCES OUTSIDE YOUR HOME 59

    FREQUENTLY ASKED QUESTIONS 62

    RECOMMENDED RESOURCES 64

3 - HEATING, COOLING, ... 66

COOKING, AND LIGHTING..66

HEATING 68

COOLING..72

COOKING 74

LIGHTING 80

FREQUENTLY ASKED QUESTIONS 89

RECOMMENDED RESOURCES 91

4 - HYGIENE...93

BATHING, DISH WASHING, AND LAUNDRY 94

WASH-WATER RECYCLNG SYSTEM..................................95

FREQUENTLY ASKED QUESTIONS 102

RECOMMENDED RESOURCES 103

5 - First Aid...105

FIRST AID KIT 131

HEALTH CARE TIPS 134

RECOMMENDED RESOURCES 135

6 - FINANCES...137

FINANCIAL SURVIVAL 142

RECOMMENDED RESOURCES 150

7 - MISCELLANEOUS MATTERS 152

    HOME SECURITY 152

    TRANSPORTATION 156

    COMMUNICATION 161

    ENTERTAINMENT 163

    ATTITUDE 166

    RECOMMENDED RESOURCES 168

8 - DOCUMENTS, RECORDS AND CHECKLISTS 170

    RECOMMENDED RESOURCES 176

IN CONCLUSION 178

INTRODUCTION

"A lot of people who are worrying about the future ought to be preparing for it."
- Anonymous

Financial crashes are nothing new. They happen over and over again. There have been 5 major crashes since the United States was founded, and 47 recessions.

As I write this book in the fall of 2020, we're on the brink of a financial crisis that could rival the Great Depression of 1929.

The corona virus has taken more than 2 million lives worldwide, and more than 350 thousand lives in the US alone, causing nearly 100 thousand businesses to shut down.

More than 21 million US workers have lost their jobs in the US in just the last few months. The official unemployment rate in the US is the highest it's been since the Great Depression.

Some of the largest and oldest companies, such as J.C. Penney, Hertz, and Neiman Marcus, have filed for bankruptcy, leaving tens-of-thousands of employees without a job.

Worldwide debt is more than $253 trillion. The US national debt has skyrocketed to $23 trillion. In order to pay off that debt every American tax payer would have to fork over $175 thousand to the IRS.

Total US consumer debt is $4 trillion. That includes mortgages, auto loans, credit cards and student loans. And 40% of all Americans don't have $400 in their bank to cover an emergency, or pay their bills should they lose their job.

We're in debt up to our eyeballs, and it's only the beginning. Worse times are yet to come.

The best advice anyone can give you is to hope for the best, but prepare for the worst, and this is the book that will show you how to do it - simply, safely, and cheaply.

I've lived through hurricanes, earthquakes, monsoons, and blizzards. While in the US Air Force, I had extensive courses in survival techniques, plus first aid and rescue techniques.

I also spent a lot of time bivouacking in the bush and putting that knowledge to good use. During my seven years in the Alaskan wilderness, I learned how to live off the land, store foods, obtain and purify water, cook with wood and gas stoves, and keep warm.

For the last 30 years I've taught people how to buy and store survival food, water, and equipment, and how to use those supplies. In this book I'll show you:

- The essential items you must have to survive this financial crisis.
- How to create a long-term food storage system that averages less than a dollar a meal.
- How to protect your money in the event of bank closures or a stock market crash.
- Easy and delicious survival-food recipes that take less than 20 minutes to prepare.
- Low cost and no-cost ways to stay warm if the electricity goes out in the winter.
- Simple, inexpensive ways to stay cool in the summer.

- The simplest and cheapest ways to cook your food and light your home.
- Emergency survival charts and checklists.
- A complete first aid guide that could save your life, or the life of a loved one.
- The one investment that could make you 200% to 500% during a financial crisis.
- A $25 first aid kit that will see you through 95% of all medical emergencies.
- How to keep financial and medical records safe.
- A list of essential suppliers, books, and internet sites to help you survive.

Survive The Coming Financial Crash Simply, Safely, And Cheaply, is a no-nonsense guide that gives you step-by-step instructions on how to protect yourself and your family from the impending financial meltdown. It could be the most important book you ever buy.

I hope this book will give you the information and the confidence to survive this financial crisis, or any other crisis, that may come your way.

- 1 -

SURVIVAL FOOD

"It wasn't raining when Noah built the ark. The best time to store food is always NOW. Now, while it is available. Now, while the food lines are shorter. Now, while there is still time."

- Perma Pak Bulletin

A few months ago, when you walked down the aisles of any supermarket, it looked like we had an abundance of food. Bins were loaded with fruits and vegetables, shelves were overflowing with cans, boxes, and bags of food, freezers were crammed with TV dinners, pizzas, ice cream, and desserts.

But now, thanks to COVID-19 taking out food workers in various sectors of the food industry, we're beginning to see food shortages.

Beyond what you see at your local supermarket, how much food do you think we have in reserve?

The surprising fact is that in the last few years our food reserves have dwindled to next to nothing. Thanks to changes in the weather, new waves of crop diseases, and the exportation of our food reserves to Russia, China, and a host of Third World countries, our food reserves are the lowest they've been in 50 years.

Our supermarkets have only a 3 -5-day reserve of food on hand, and the industries that supply them - farming, processing, packaging, and trucking - are at risk. One or two broken links in the long chain of industries that bring us the food we eat, and we'll be in big trouble.

So, what do you do? How do you protect yourself and your family from starvation if food supplies run out or can't be trucked in to your local supermarket? The simple solution is if you can't grow it, *store it*.

THE CANNED AND DRIED FOOD STORAGE PLAN

The best food storage system is one that is simple, easy, inexpensive, and allows you to eat what you want. The canned and dried food plan is just that. It's the plan my wife, Grace, and I have been using for years and we love it. Here's why:

It's cheap. Using canned and dried foods for emergency food as well as for our daily meals, Grace and I spend about $45 a week for the two of us. That's $3 per person per day to eat, drink, and even have dessert.

It's tastes good. The first rule of any good food storage plan is to have foods you already enjoy eating.

I've read a number of reports about people in survival situations who ended up starving rather than eat the food they had on hand just because they couldn't stand the taste. Having food that tastes good, and food you're used to eating, isn't just a luxury, it's a necessity.

It took Grace and me a couple of months to create and refine the recipes we now enjoy, but it was well worth it. When Grace and I serve our "survival food" dinners to friends and family we get rave reviews. We have the pleasure of knowing that in a survival situation we won't be just subsisting, we'll be feasting!

It's convenient. Before we used this food storage system, we would spend an inordinate amount of time, at least two or three times a week, running to our local supermarket for food we'd run out of, food we had a craving for, or food we'd forgotten to get.

Now we shop for food only once a week. Figuring that it takes us about half-an-hour to travel to-and-from our house, and another half-hour to shop, we figure we save about 12 hours a month. That's an extra day every month we can do something we enjoy instead of grocery shopping.

Grace and I also love the convenience of opening our food closet to get something we ran out of, instead of driving our car all the way to the supermarket, wandering the aisles until we find what we need, standing in line at the checkout counter, then driving all the way home.

Another advantage, especially in survival circumstances where fuel and water are at a premium, is you can eat most canned foods right out of the can without adding water or heating them.

It's healthy. Knowing that in a survival situation you'll have to depend on your food to maintain your health, you tend to shop for healthier food than you normally would. Also, shopping only once a week with a list cuts down on junk-food impulse buying.

Processed food has received a lot of bad press over the years because most writers have assumed that "fresh" fruit and vegetables and "unprocessed" meat and fish are better for you. Not always the case.

Recently it was discovered that many canned fruits and vegetables retain more of their vitamins and nutrients than "fresh" ones.

The reason? Vegetables left out in the open quickly lose their nutrients. After fruits and vegetables are picked, they may spend days in boxes waiting to be shipped to your supermarket. Once there, they'll spend even more time sitting out in the open until you take them home. Once home, you may wait days until you eat them.

Canned fruits and vegetables, on the other hand, lose their nutrients much less slowly and retain those nutrients until you open them

You may have noticed that most of the recent E Coli outbreaks have come from "fresh," not canned, meat and vegetables. The canning process destroys harmful bacteria and viruses that cause major illnesses.

It gives you peace of mind. I'm truly amazed at the number of people I know who are preparing for the worst by hoarding money and precious metals, thinking they'll be able to buy food when the stuff hits the fan.

Wrong! You can't eat gold coins. And I have it on good authority that greenbacks are not exactly a culinary delight either. Having all the money in the world won't prevent you from starving if there isn't any food to buy.

 Our supermarkets have only a three-day reserve of food, and only three hours in an emergency situation.

I remember surviving a hurricane in Miami Florida. A few hours after the alarm was sounded the grocery store shelves were cleaned out. Storing food now is the only way you can be sure you'll have it when you need it.

And after the crash subsides, you'll have food on hand that will allow you to survive future disasters like hurricanes, tornadoes, floods, and power outages, and to get through future emergencies such as losing your job, or not being unable to work due to ill health or an accident.

A few years back I lost my business due to an economic downturn. I lived for two months on the food I had stored until I got back on my feet. After that, I became a firm believer in always having food in reserve.

OUR PERSONAL STORAGE PLAN

Years ago, after reading a number of books on long-term food storage, I decided that most of the systems I'd read about were either too expensive, too complicated, or depended on food I wouldn't eat in a million years. So, I decided to create my own system based on the foods I lived on in the Alaskan wilderness and foods I took with me when I went camping.

I began by making a list of all the foods I liked best. After doing research on what foods would retain their food value and still taste good after an extended period of time, I was shocked to learn that I could use only three of my original twenty favorite recipes.

Thinking there had to be a way I could use substitute foods to create meals I would enjoy, I went down to my library and got my hands on everything I could find on food storage, camping foods, and cooking.

After many months of experimenting with recipes and long-term storage foods, Grace and I created a number of dishes that not only tasted good, they were quick to make, and were cheap.

I discovered that between the freeze-dried food we purchased online, and the canned and packaged food we got from the grocery store, getting the food we needed was relatively easy and inexpensive. I also discovered that some of the food I had grown to hate in the Air Force - namely powdered milk, eggs, and cheese - had gone through some changes and were not only edible, they actually tasted good.

In order to keep our survival food system simple, Grace and I decided to limit our breakfast and lunch recipes, and use just 15 recipes for dinner. It sounded drastic to us at the time, but now that we've been eating a relatively simple diet, we wouldn't have it any other way.

For breakfast we eat either a granola-type cereal with raisins, Cheerios with honey, oatmeal with raisins and maple syrup, Cream of Wheat with Craisins (dried cranberries), or scrambled eggs and pancakes. If we're hungry for a snack, we'll have some crackers, peanuts, cashews, or dried fruit.

For lunch, we'll eat a peanut butter and jelly sandwich, crackers and cheese, a bean burrito, a cheese quesadilla (tortilla with melted cheese), or Spanish rice and beans.

For dinner we enjoy either a steaming plate of spaghetti topped with cheese, eggs with pancakes and maple syrup, Grace's famous macaroni and cheese, buttered rice and black beans, soup (minestrone, vegetable, mushroom or tomato) with a cheese sandwich, Boston baked beans and cornbread, a Spanish omelet, Spanish rice and beans, a bean burrito with red rice, Ramen with veggies or lentils, vegetable stir fry, or a bowl of chili topped with cheese sauce.

For dessert we enjoy cinnamon/honey graham crackers, cookies, dried fruit, apple sauce, canned peaches, canned mixed fruit, a bowl of buttered popcorn, hot chocolate with marshmallows, or some M&M's.

We do eat fresh vegetables and food from our fridge, but the bulk of our meals is from our survival pantry.

Another plus to the food storage system Grace and I created is all of the recipes take less than 30 minutes to cook. I love to eat, but I hate to cook.

After we refined our recipes, I wrote them down and downloaded them into my cell phone. All we have to do to fix a meal is turn on my cell phone and follow the recipe. A real no brainer.

Note: A few years ago, Grace and I became vegetarian, so we've included both vegetarian and the non-vegetarian recipes we created, like roast beef and mashed potatoes, and chicken and tomato rice.

The key to using this type of system for any period of time is rotation. You have to use the food you store and replenish it at regular intervals. At the end of this chapter there's a shelf life chart that shows the length of time certain foods can be stored.

To figure out how much food you need to store using our recipes, multiply the ingredients times the number of people in your family.

Here are a few of our favorite recipes:

CANNED-AND-DRIED FOOD RECIPES

Bean Burritos and Rice (2 servings)

4 tortillas
16 ounce can refried beans
3/4 tablespoon dried minced onions
1/8 cup cold water

- Put minced onions into a cup with water to rehydrate.
- After 10 minutes, mix onions and beans, put into pot and warm on medium heat.

3/8 cup rehydrated freeze-dried cheese

3/8 cup hot water
4 tablespoons salsa or picante sauce

- Mix cheese and water until smooth.
- Warm burrito in a pan.
- Put refried beans, cheese and salsa on tortilla, fold up the ends, then roll up into a burrito.

1/2 cup rice
1 cup water
1-1/2 tablespoons rehydrated freeze-dried butter

1/2 teaspoons salt

- Put ingredients in medium pot.
- Bring to boil, cover pot, then simmer 15 to 25 minutes depending on type of rice.
- Fluff rice, then let stand 5 minutes.
- Spread butter on rice.

Variations: Top rice with salsa. Serve with tortilla chips and salsa, or cheese. Add 2 cups chicken or beef bouillon to pot before cooking.

Biscuits (6 biscuits)

1 cup biscuit mix
3/8 cup rehydrated dried milk

- Mix ingredients with fork until dough leaves side of bowl (add extra biscuit mix if needed).
- Using a spoon, drop dough balls onto large, preheated (medium), lightly oiled pan.
- Bake 5 to 7 minutes or until brown, then turn biscuits over with spatula and repeat.

Variations: Serve with butter, jelly, peanut butter, or honey. Substitute pancake
mix for biscuit mix.

No Knead Bread (1 loaf)

13 ounces warm (not hot) water
1-1/2 teaspoons salt
1-1/2 teaspoons dry yeast (packages are 2 1/4 to 2 1/2 teaspoons)
2 teaspoons oil
3-1/2 cups bread flour or all-purpose flour

- Mix water, yeast, salt, and oil in bowl until yeast and salt are dissolved.
- Let rest for 5 minutes to activate yeast.
- Add flour and mix until flour is totally moistened from water.
- Cover bowl with plastic wrap and let rise in a warm location for 1-1/2 hours or until doubled in size.

- Preheat oven to 400 degrees.
- Gently deflate the dough by the folding dough over on itself a few times.
- Coat a baking pan with oil.
- Roll the dough out of the bowl and into a 9 X 5 bread pan, spreading it out to fill the pan with a spatula or large spoon.
- Cover the pan and allow dough to rise again until the has risen to almost the top of the baking pan (about 30 minutes).
- Bake at 400 degrees for 40 minutes or until golden brown.
- Take the bread out of the oven and let cool for 30 minutes.

Variations: Add 1 tablespoon of sugar or 2 teaspoons of honey to help the bread rise. Spread on butter, cinnamon sugar, honey, or peanut butter and jelly. Make a sandwich with sliced Spam and mayonnaise, deviled ham, Vienna sausage, tuna salad, chicken salad, scrambled eggs and mayonnaise, or roast beef and barbecue sauce.

Cheese Omelet (2 servings)

3/8 cup rehydrated freeze-dried cheese
1/2 cup hot water

- Mix cheese blend and water until smooth.

3/4 cup dried egg mix
1 cup water
3 teaspoons oil

- Coat pan with oil and preheat on medium heat.
- Mix eggs and water, then pour egg mix into pan and turn heat to low.
- Cook eggs, lifting edges of omelet with a spatula to allow uncooked portion to run to bottom of skillet.
- When mixture is set, but top is still moist, pour cheese blend into one half of omelet.
- Loosen edge of omelet, fold in half, then slide into serving plate and cover.

Variations: Spread salsa inside omelet for a Spanish omelet. Fill omelet with Spam chunks for a ham omelet, or the vegetable of your choosing for a vegetable omelet.

Chicken & Tomato Rice (2 servings)

14.5 ounces canned diced tomatoes
5 ounces canned chicken
2/3 cup rice
1 cup water
1-1/2 tablespoons minced onions
1 teaspoon sugar
1/2 teaspoon salt
1/4 teaspoon granulated garlic
1-1/2 teaspoons chicken bouillon
1 tablespoon rehydrated freeze-dried butter

- Mix ingredients in medium pot, then bring to boil.
- Turn heat to medium/low, cover, and simmer for 25 minutes.
- Remove from heat, stir, then let stand 5 minutes.

Variations: Serve with crackers, tortillas, bread, or canned or dehydrated
beans, corn, or the vegetable of your choice.

Chicken Noodle Soup (2 servings)

6 ounces canned chicken
14.5 oz. canned mixed vegetables
4 ounces egg noodles
1 tablespoon onion flakes
1 teaspoon chicken bouillon
1/2 teaspoon salt
1/2 teaspoon sugar
1/3 teaspoon garlic powder

- Mix ingredients in medium pot, then bring to boil.
- Cover pot, then simmer soup on medium heat for 15 minutes.
- Serve with crackers and cheese.

Variations: Serve with tortilla chips and salsa, or serve with bread and butter.

Chili with Rice

15 ounce can chili
15 ounce can chopped tomatoes
1/2 cup rice
1 tablespoon rehydrated dried chopped onions
1/2 teaspoon salt
1 tablespoon butter
1/2 teaspoon salt
2 teaspoons olive oil

3/8 cup rehydrated freeze-dried cheese
1/4 cup water

- Drain chopped tomato juice into measuring cup, then add water until you have 3/4 cup of liquid.
- Put liquid into a pot with rice and onions, bring to a boil, the simmer for 15 minutes.
- Add remaining ingredients into pot and heat until ingredients are warm.
- Sprinkle cheese over chile.

Variations: Serve with bread, or tortillas.

Cornbread (4 servings)

7-1/2 ounces cornbread mix
1-1/2 cups rehydrated dry milk

- Blend cornbread mix and milk in a small bowl until smooth.
- Pour mixture into a small (8" diameter), lightly oil pan.
- Cover and cook on low heat for 20 to 25 minutes.

Variations: Serve with butter, honey, maple syrup, or jelly. Add dried hot pepper pieces to mix for spicy cornbread.

Flat Bread (6 servings)

1-1/2 cups pancake mix
1-1/3 cups water
1/2 teaspoon salt
1 teaspoon sugar or 1/2 teaspoon honey

- Blend pancake mix and water with fork, leaving slightly lumpy.
- Pour 5" pancakes into pan and cook until bubbles form.
- Turn pancake over, then cook until golden brown.
- Repeat process for remaining five pancakes.
- Air dry for 4 hours before putting into container to store.

Variations: Substitute buttermilk or whole wheat pancake mix for regular pancake mix. Flat bread tastes good with butter, cinnamon sugar, honey, or peanut butter and jelly.

Macaroni and Cheese (2 servings)

1-1/2 cup macaroni or rotini
4 tablespoons rehydrated freeze-dried butter
1 cup rehydrated freeze-dried cheese
1/4 cup rehydrated dry milk
8.5 ounces canned peas

- Rehydrate butter and cheese according to directions
- Boil water in medium pot.
- Stir in macaroni and boil until tender (7-10 minutes).
- Drain macaroni in a colander and return to pot.
- Put cheese, milk, and butter in a small pot, heat on low, and mix until blended.
- Add peas and blended cheese to macaroni and mix in thoroughly.

Variations: Add one small can of tuna. Substitute the vegetable of your choice for
peas. Serve with bread or tortillas.

Quesadilla

1/4 cup rehydrated freeze-dried cheese
1 tortilla

- Sprinkle cheese on half of a tortilla and fold in half.
- Fry tortilla on medium heat for 30 seconds or until cheese melts.
- Dip tortilla in salsa or picante sauce.

Ramen Noodles and Lentils

15-ounce can of Lentil soup
Two packages of chicken or beef Ramen noodles

- Open and drain water from lentil soup.
- Heat lentil soup until warm.
- Bring 2 cups of water to a boil in a pot.
- Add noodles and cook for 3 minutes, stirring occasionally.
- Pour noodles into a colander to drain them.
- Sprinkle flavor packets over noodles and mix them in.
- Put noodles on plates and pour lentils over them.

Variations: Substitute your favorite canned veggies for lentils and season with soy sauce. Serve with rolls or bread.

Rice and Black Beans

15-ounce canned black beans
1\8 cup water
1/2 tablespoon minced onions
1 tablespoon vegetable oil

1/4 teaspoon garlic powder
1/4 teaspoon cumin (optional)

- Mix all ingredients in a small pot.
- Bring to boil, cover pot, then simmer on low heat for 30 minutes.

2/3 cup rice
1-1/3 cup water
2 tablespoons rehydrated freeze-dried butter
2/3 teaspoons salt

- Put ingredients in medium pot.
- Bring to boil, cover pot, then simmer 15 to 25 minutes depending on type of rice.
- Fluff rice, then let stand 5 minutes.

Variations: Top rice or beans with salsa. Serve with the canned vegetable of your choice. Serve with tortilla chips and salsa or bread.

Tortillas (12 tortillas)

2 cups all-purpose flour
3 tablespoon oil
1/2 teaspoon salt
3/4 cups warm water

- In a large bowl, combine flour and salt, then stir in water and oil.
- Turn onto a floured surface, knead 10 to 12 times, adding a little flour or water if needed for a smooth dough.
- Let rest for 10 minutes.

- Divide dough into 8 portions, then on a lightly floured surface, roll each portion into a 7-inch circle.
- Cook tortillas over medium heat in a greased skillet until lightly browned, 1 minute on each side.

Variations: Tortillas taste good with butter, honey, cinnamon sugar, jelly, or peanut butter.

Pancakes and Scrambled Eggs (2 servings)

1-1/2 cups pancake mix
1-1/4 cups water
1/3 cup maple syrup
2 teaspoons oil

- Preheat griddle on medium/high for 3 minutes.
- Blend pancake mix and water with fork, leaving slightly lumpy.
- Pour batter on lightly oiled pan, cook until bubbles appear.
- Turn pancake over and cook until light brown.

3/4 cup dried egg mix
1 cup water

Mix eggs and water, then cook to desired firmness in lightly buttered pan.

2 tablespoons freeze-dried butter
1 tablespoon water
1 tablespoon vegetable oil

- Mix butter, water, and oil in a cup until smooth, then spread on pancakes.

Variations: Serve with thin-sliced cooked Spam or dehydrated hash brown potatoes.

Individual Pizzas

8 ounce can tomato sauce
6 slices of bread
1 cup rehydrated freeze-dried cheese
1/2 teaspoon Italian seasoning
1/8 teaspoon salt
1/8 teaspoon granulated garlic

- Preheat oven to 425 degrees.
- Mix Italian seasoning, salt, and garlic into tomato sauce.
- Spread sauce on bread then cover with cheese.
- Bake for 5 minutes or until cheese is melted.

Rice and Vegetables (2 servings)

3/4 cup rice
1-1/2 cups water
3/4 teaspoons salt
2 teaspoons chicken bouillon
1 tablespoon butter

- Mix ingredients in small pot, cover, then bring to boil.
- Simmer 15 to 25 minutes (depending on type of rice) on low heat, fluff, then let stand 5 minutes.

14.5 ounces canned mixed vegetables
1 tablespoon rehydrated freeze-dried butter

- Put vegetables in small pot, heat until warm, mix into rice or spoon on top of rice, then spread butter on vegetables.

Variations: Pour soy sauce, or sweet and sour sauce over rice.
Substitute dehydrated vegetable of your choosing for mixed vegetables.

Roast Beef and Mashed Potatoes, and Corn (2 servings)

12 ounces canned roast beef
1/2 teaspoon onion powder
1/4 teaspoon granulated garlic
1/8 teaspoon cumin

Mix ingredients in small pot and warn on medium heat.

1 cup potato flakes
1cup water
3/8 cup dry milk
2-1/2 tablespoons butter
3/8 teaspoons salt

- Mix water, butter, and salt in medium pot, boil, then remove from heat.
- Add milk, then gently stir in potato flakes.

Variations: For barbecued roast beef, drain gravy from roast beef and substitute barbecue sauce. Add canned corn, peas, mixed vegetables, carrots, or the vegetable of your choice. Serve Roast beef with rice or Ramen noodles instead of potatoes.

Shepherd's Pie (2 servings)

3/4 cup potato flakes
1-1/2 cups water

- Boil water in medium skillet.
- Stir in ingredients, then cook until light brown.

24 ounces canned beef stew
1 tablespoon onion flakes
1/2 teaspoon sugar
1/2 teaspoon salt
1/4 teaspoon garlic powder

- Mix ingredients in medium pot.
- Warm on medium heat, then spoon stew on top of potatoes.

Variations: Serve with bread, canned beans, peas, corn, or the vegetable of your choice.

Spaghetti

15 oz can tomato sauce
3 tablespoons rehydrated dried bell peppers
2 tablespoons rehydrated dry chopped onions
1 teaspoon Italian seasoning
1/4 teaspoon salt
1/4 teaspoon granulated garlic

- Mix ingredients in pot, cover, then heat on low for 20 minutes.

6 ounces spaghetti
2 tablespoons rehydrated freeze-dried butter

3 tablespoons rehydrated freeze-dried cheese
3 cups water

- Boil water in medium pot, then add spaghetti.
- Turn heat to medium and boil until tender (7-12 minutes depending on type of spaghetti).
- Spread butter on noodles, top with spaghetti sauce and cheese.

Variations: Add 1 small can chicken, Vienna sausages, or 1/4 cup rehydrated beef flavored TVP to spaghetti sauce. Serve with bread and/or the canned or dehydrated vegetable of your choice.

EAT WHAT YOU LIKE

The preceding recipes give you an idea of how to use canned and dehydrated storage foods to create a variety of tasty and nutritious recipes.

The key to a good storage program is to create recipes you will want to eat, rather than have to eat.

To create a survival food system similar to ours you first need to write down what you normally eat. Think about the things you and your family eat on a daily basis. Do the foods you now enjoy store without refrigeration? Can you think of ways to recreate the meals you enjoy by substituting canned and dried foods?

Use a cook book or go online to a recipe site to discover what substitutes you can make in your recipes, and what new recipes you might enjoy that include canned and dehydrated ingredients.

Remember to keep it simple. A couple of breakfast recipes, a few lunches, and 10 to 15 dinner recipes is all you need for a complete food storage system with enough variety to keep you and your family happy. Keep in mind you're trying to create simple, good-tasting recipes, not compete with the chef Ramsey.

When you have a list of your favorite foods, use the following shelf-life chart as a guide, along with your imagination, to see what canned and dehydrated food products you can use as is, and which ones you can use as substitutions for your favorite recipes.

SHELF LIFE

Beans, Flours, Grains, and Pasta

Beans (dried)—2 years
Biscuit Mix—2 years
Cake Mixes—2 years
Corn (dried)—10 years
Cornmeal—5 years
Crackers—10 months
Flour (white)—1 year
Hardtack—25 years
Macaroni—5 years
Muffin Mix—2 years
Noodles—5 years
Oatmeal—2 years
Pancake Mix—2 years
Pasta—20 years
Ramen—10 years
Rice (brown)—12 months
Rice (white)—20 years
Wheat—12 years

Condiments and Cooking Aids

Arrow Root—2 years
Baking Powder—1 year
Baking Soda—indefinite
Bouillon—10 years

Catsup—3 years
Cornstarch—5 years
Gelatin—3 years
Gravy Mix (canned)—2 years
Gravy Mix (powdered)—4 years
Maple Flavoring—3 years
Maple Syrup—indefinite
Mayonnaise—1 year
Molasses—2-1/2 years
Olive Oil—3 years
Pepper—indefinite
Relish—indefinite
Salad Dressings—1 year
Salt—indefinite
Shortening—1-1/2 years
Soy Sauce—indefinite
Sour Dough Starter—indefinite
Spices (ground)—2-1/2 years
Spices (whole)—5 years
TVP (box)—3years
TVP (vacuum packed) —5 years
Vanilla extract—indefinite
Vegetable Oil—2 years
Vinegar—indefinite
Worcestershire Sauce—indefinite
Yeast (powdered)—1-1/2 years

Canned Meat

Beef—2 years
Beef (chipped)—2 years
Chicken—2 years
Clams—2 years
Crab—2 years

Deviled Ham—2 years
Roast Beef—2 years
Shrimp (canned)—2 years
Salmon—2 years
Sardines—3 years
Tuna Fish—2 years
Turkey—2 years
Vienna Sausage—2 years

Dairy Foods

Butter (dehydrated)—8 years
Buttermilk (dehydrated)—5 years
Cheese (dehydrated)—8years
Chocolate Drink Mix—2 years
Eggs (dehydrated, canned)—8 years
Milk (dehydrated, canned)—20 years
Milk (evaporated)—3 years
Milk (powdered)—20 years
Velveeta—6 months

Drinks

Alcohol—indefinite
Apple Juice—2 years
Apricot Juice—1 year
Cocoa—2 years
Coffee—2 years
Cream (non-dairy) —3 years
Drink Mixes (powdered) —5 years
Grape Juice—2 years
Grapefruit Juice—1 year
Pineapple Juice—1 year

Prune Juice—2 years
Soft Drinks—1-1/2 years
Tea (bags)—3 years
Tea (instant)—5 years
Tomato Juice—3 years

Fruits and Vegetables

Asparagus (canned)—3 years
Beans (canned)—3 years
Beans (dried)—10 years
Beets (canned)—2 years
Carrots (canned)—3 years
Carrots (dehydrated) —5 years
Corn (canned)—3 years
Fruits (canned)—2 years
Fruit (citrus, canned)—1 year
Fruits (dried) —1 year
Green Beans (canned)—3 years
Green Beans (dried) —5 years
Mixed Vegetables (canned)—3 years
Nuts (canned)—2 years
Nuts (unshelled)—2 years
Olives (canned)—3 years
Peas (canned)—3 years
Peas (dried)—1O years
Pickles—indefinite
Potatoes (dehydrated)—20 years
Potato Flakes—15 years
Tomatoes (canned)—3 years
Tomatoes (paste/sauce)—3 years
Vegetables (mixed, dried)—4 years

Snacks, Sweets, and Desserts

Cake Mix—2 years
Candy (bars)—1-1/2 years
Candy (hard)—2 years
Corn Syrup—indefinite
Cookies—1-1/2 years
Corn chips—1-1/2 years
Crackers—1-1/2 years
Graham Crackers—2 years
Honey (diluted)—5 years
Honey (undiluted)—Indefinite
Jell-O—indefinitely
Popcorn (un-popped)—1O years
Potato Chips—1-1/2 years
Puddings (mixes)—3 year
Puddings (premixed)—2 years
Sugar (brown)—indefinite
Sugar (maple)—5 years
Sugar (white)—indefinite

Miscellaneous

Baby Food—1 year
Baby Formula—1-1/2 years
Breakfast Cereals—1-1/2 years
Coffee—6 months
Coffee (instant)—10 years
Jam—2 years
Jelly—2 years
Mineral Supplements—2 years
Peanut Butter—2 years
Pet Food (canned) —2 years
Pet Food (dried)—1-1/2 years

Soups (canned)—3 years
Soups (dried)—2-1/2 years
Spaghetti Sauce—2 years
Vitamin Supplements—2 years

The above shelf life information is based on the average maximum storage times for foods stored in unopened containers at an average temperature of 70⁰ F, kept dry and out of direct light. Actual storage times will vary according to storage conditions and type of container used.

Multivitamin/Mineral Supplements

The old school of thought on vitamin and mineral supplements was if you ate a variety of foods, you'd get more than enough vitamins and minerals. The new school of thought is that because we're depleting the soil in which our food is grown, and because most of us tend to be junk food junkies, supplements are a must for good health.

The healthiest people I know are the ones who eat lots or veggies, fruits, nuts, and grains, and are taking vitamin and mineral supplements. Happily, Grace and I are members of that group. We take a combination multi-vitamin/mineral supplement, along with vitamin C and magnesium. Neither one of us has had a major illness, or even a minor one for that matter, in years.

How Much to Store

Grace and I keep a six-month supply of food stored in our in our kitchen cupboards and around the house. We also store buckets of grains and beans to feed family and friends who may not have put food aside. How much food you store depends on what you think will happen.

If you think financial crisis is just going to cause sporadic problems that won't last long, then I suggest buying a food supply that will last a minimum of one month, preferably two months.

If you think the financial crisis is going to last for an indefinite period of time, I suggest you get a four-to-twelve-month supply of food for you and your family. Four months' worth of food should give you enough time to start a garden and be eating from it when your food supplies run out. Even if nothing happens, you'll have extra food on hand for other emergencies.

If your resources are limited, start small. Purchase an extra one or two weeks' worth of food next time you go shopping, and build from there. It will cost less than $25 per person per week using canned and dried foods.

Because you'll be eating your emergency food, your money won't be wasted. Fact is, you'll actually be saving money. That, plus the peace of mind you'll gain having food on hand to see you through hard times will be well worth your time and effort.

STORAGE CHECKLIST

- Store bulk food in rodent-proof metal cans, or heavy-duty, plastic containers, with air-tight lids. Do not use containers that have contained toxic materials or have a strong odor, and make sure containers are clean. Close containers tightly after opening.
- Most canned goods are good for up to 2 years beyond their expiration date, but the lose a little nutritional value after that time.
- Check cans for bulges (could mean botulism poisoning), and check contents for spoilage (if it smells bad it probably is bad). When in doubt, toss it out!
- Store all containers off cement or dirt floors to prevent moisture infiltration and rust. Put containers on wood, cardboard, or on shelves.
- Store your food in a coolest, driest part of your house, in an area that's dark—a closet or a room on the north side of your house, covered shelves on the north side of your

garage, your basement, under your bed, or the lowest cupboards in your kitchen.

- Rotate your food supplies - store what you eat and eat what you store. This is the key to maintaining a safe and nutritious food storage plan.

- Store your food by grouping the same food items together. Place newly purchased food at the back of the shelf, moving older items forward to be used first.

FREQUENTLY ASKED QUESTIONS

I already have a lot of frozen food. Can't I just get some more of it and store it in my freezer?

Using refrigeration as a means to store food has a number of drawbacks: 1) frozen food is generally more expensive than canned and dried food, 2) the electricity to run a refrigerator or freezer adds $100 to $200 a year to your initial food cost, 3) most refrigerated and frozen foods don't last that long (2 to 6 months on average), 4) if the electricity in your area were to go out for a period of time, you'd eventually end up with a smelly mass of rotting food.

Since Grace and I discovered the joys of canned and dried food, we don't keep a lot of food in our refrigerator. If the electricity goes out, food kept in a refrigerator with the door closed will last only 2 or 3 days, so we'll use that food first, then go back to eating our canned and dried foods.

I don't have much money. What can I do to put together a food storage program?

Just do the best you can with what you have.

Start with water. Purchase water in 1-gallon containers. Clean old juice, soda, and water containers, and use the bleach treatment method (next chapter) to store water. When you can afford it, start buying water jugs to store water. You can survive for weeks without food if you have an adequate supply of water.

Take inventory on how much food you have in your cupboards. Then see what you can do to supplement that food with inexpensive foods like flour, grains, and beans.

Try to build up your food reserves a little at a time. The next time your go shopping buy as much extra food as you can afford. Even if you can only afford a few extra items, over time those items will add up. A one-week supply of food for a family of four, using the canned-and-dried system, costs less than $90. An extra week or two of food is better than nothing.

What about including some fresh fruits and vegetables? I know that potatoes keep for a long time.

Keeping some fresh fruits and vegetables on hand is a good idea. Just don't depend on them for long-term storage.

Here are some storage times for fruit and vegetables kept in a cool location like a basement or root cellar: carrots—2 months, green tomatoes—1 month, Onions—3 months, potatoes—3 months, squash—2 months.

Hard fruits like apples and pears will keep through fall and winter if kept in a cold basement or root cellar, or buried in the ground in a barrel.

How about hunting and fishing for food?

There's an old adage among hunters: Don't use up more energy hunting a critter than that critter will give you back.

People have died in the wilds of Canada and Alaska hunting rabbits. Rabbits don't have much fat on them and the energy expended hunting, cooking and eating them is actually less than the rabbit meat gives back to the hunter.

Unless you know what you're doing, you'll waste more time and energy hunting than it's worth.

Fishing uses less energy than hunting, but again, unless you know what you're doing, you're better off spending the money you'd spend on fishing equipment on storage food.

I live in a small apartment. Where can I store a one-year supply of food?

Start first with your cupboards. Repack food in smaller containers and get rid of food that's gone bad or food you won't eat. Then group your food by categories (canned meat, soups, vegetables etc.)

Pack empty spaces in your refrigerator with canned food. Not only will it keep longer, it will save on your electric bill by taking up unused refrigeration space.

Look for unused spaces in your home. One of the best places to store food is under your bed. If your bed is low to the ground, you can raise it by putting wood blocks or bed risers under the legs.

How about the bottoms and tops of your closets? You can store non-perishable items like blankets and clothes in your attic, then use the space they occupied to store food.

I remember eating dried eggs and powdered milk in the Army. It was lousy. Does the food you recommend taste any better?

Definitely! Newer processing techniques have made foods like dried milk, dried eggs, and dried cheese taste almost like the real thing.

What about the nutritional value of canned foods?

As my mother likes to say, "The proof is in the pudding."

I ate dehydrated foods and C rations when I was in the Air Force, and canned and dried foods when I lived in Alaska, and was as healthy as a horse. Grace and I have been eating canned and dehydrated foods for a number of years and we're two of the healthiest people we know.

Nutritional "experts" change their collective minds so often, it's hard to keep track of what they think is good for you and what's not. If you're really concerned about what nutrients you're getting from canned and dehydrated foods, read the nutritional labels on the cans and packages and create your recipes accordingly.

How about military rations? We heard something called "MRE's" are a good way to store emergency food? What are they, and are they any good?

The old C rations I ate when I was in the Air Force were godawful to say the least. The new military rations known as MRE's (Meals Ready to Eat), are almost as good as home cooking. They're really expensive, costing from $6 to $8 a meal, but as a supplement to your storage program when you can't get food like ham or bacon, they can't be beat.

If you buy MRE's, make sure you check the date marked on the carton to get the freshest food you can. MRE's have a shelf life of 5 years stored at 72-degrees.

I've seen prepackaged 1-year food supplies advertised in magazines and online. Are these any good?

The problem with most commercial food storage systems is they aren't tailored to your individual tastes. They tend to include foods that most of us wouldn't eat if we had another choice. That, and they're expensive, varying in price from $2,500 to over $3,000 per person for a one-year supply of food. That's two to three times as expensive as a canned and dehydrated food storage system.

What about using the freeze-dried foods I've seen in camping stores'?

Freeze dried foods are expensive - $4 to $6 per person per meal - and though some freeze-dried food tastes great, the portions tend to be skimpy.

However, if you have a hankering for lasagna with meat sauce, shrimp Alfredo, or a good ol' chili mac with beef, then adding some freeze-dried food to your food supplies might be a good idea.

Most camping stores, and online retailers like Amazon, carry freeze-dried food. They have a shelf life of 4 to 7 years depending on how they're stored.

I've heard that canning your own food is a cheap and easy way to store food. And what about dehydrating?

Canning is neither cheap nor easy. When you consider the initial outlay for canning supplies, plus the cost of fresh fruit, vegetables and meat, you'll find it's a lot cheaper to buy commercially canned and dried food. But if you have the necessary canning supplies and know what you're doing, it's a good way to augment your survival food supply.

The same holds true for dehydrating your food. By the time you spend $100 to $300 for a decent home dehydrator, then buy fresh food to dry, you're better off spending your money on prepackaged dried food from your supermarket.

The only reason to consider canning or dehydrating your food is if you have a garden and want to can your surplus vegetables, or if you like the taste of particular foods and can't find them already canned or dehydrated.

How about foraging for food?

If you want to play Euell Gibbons and run around your neighborhood picking dandelions, chickweed, and cattails, by all means do so. I do it all the time. But if you're serious about surviving, you'll forage for food only as a last resort.

Even when you know what you're doing, it's just not worth the time and energy.

How long will the food in my refrigerator last if the power goes out?

Depending on the type of food, it will last anywhere from 2 to 3 days if you keep your frig door closed. In an emergency, use the food in your fridge first. Take out the food you need quickly and try not to open the door too often.

RECOMMENDED RESOURCES

Visit **www.frugalsurvivalist.com** for information about the products listed below or to purchase them:

Can rack organizer

Dried and freeze-dried food

Easy-to-use can opener

Mixing pitcher

STORAGE CLOSET WITH SIX-MONTH FOOD SUPPLY FOR TWO PEOPLE

Our survival food storage shelves hold our canned goods, spices, vitamins, water jugs, freeze-dried food, dry packaged food, drink mixes, syrup, oil, rice, and beans.

- 2 -

WATER

"When the well is dry, we know the worth of water."
- Benjamin Franklin

STORE WATER NOW!

That being said, let me explain why: Water, something we take for granted, is our most precious resource. You can live for three weeks without food, but you can live for only 3 days without water.

The pumps that pump water from the ground into your home require electricity to operate. The pumps that pump water from the ground into your home require electricity to operate. If the power grid in your area were to go down, or your water company were to go broke, you would eventually be without water. If you didn't have another source of water, you'd be in big trouble.

The average person in the USA. uses more than 150 gallons of water a day to drink, bathe, wash clothes, do dishes, flush toilets, water the lawn, and so on. Fortunately, you don't need 150 gallons a day to survive. You can survive, and survive in style, on Just 1 gallon of water a day. I know, I've done it.

When I lived in Alaska, I got my water from a stream 300 yards from my cabin. Because I had to lug my water in two 5-gallon G.I. cans, and because I had to melt snow in the winter when the ice was too thick to chop through, I learned how to conserve water. Once I got used to it, it wasn't all that bad. In the Hygiene section of this book I'll show you how to take a bath with just a quart of water.

Water can carry some of the nastiest and deadliest diseases known to man.

In North America one of the most common drinking water problems is giardiasis, caused by a parasite that breeds in the intestines and multiplies into millions of new parasites.

Giardiasis is characterized by acute diarrhea, cramping, bloating, burping, gas, and anorexia. People who contract Giardiasis experience such acute stomach problems and weight loss they are sometimes hospitalized.

In South America, amebic dysentery (a.k.a. "Montezuma's Revenge" and "The Turista Two-Step"), contracted from drinking water, takes its toll on tens-of thousands of unwary tourists, and in severe cases can cause death.

Water, our most precious resource, can also be our greatest enemy. But properly treated it can easily be made safe. Here's how:

WATER TREATMENT GUDE

Bleach Method

1 quart - use 2 drops of bleach
1 gallon - use 6 drops of bleach
5 gallons - use 1/3 teaspoon of bleach

- Use unscented household bleach (without phosphates) containing at least 6 % chlorine that's less than a year old.
- Pour a little water into your container, add the proper amount of bleach, then fill the container with water. The rushing action of the water entering the container should

be enough to mix the bleach and water, but shake the container a few times to make sure.
- Let the water stand for a couple of hours, with the lid off the container, before you drink it to lessen the chlorine taste.

Note: This is a good way to treat large amounts of water. Bleach is cheap and treating water this way is easy.

Boiling Method

- Boil water in a pot or large metal container for at least 10 minutes.
- Pour back and forth between two containers to aerate and eliminate flat taste.

Note: This is the safest way to treat large quantities of water, other than water that's chemically toxic, but it's also the most time consuming.

Filter Method

- Place water-filter tube into your water source.
- Pump water into container (takes about 1 minute to get 1 quart of treated water).

Note: Water filters will get rid of most of the bacteria, viruses, and protozoa that contaminate water, but not all of them. If you suspect fecal contamination in the water you're going to filter, treat the water with iodine first, or use a water purifier with a .02-micron filter.

Due to their high initial cost - $25 to $130 plus the cost of filter replacement - water filters are a fairly expensive way to treat water. However, they do improve the taste of polluted water and are a convenient way to treat small quantities of water.

Iodine Tablet Method

1 quart - 2 tablets
1 gallon - 4 tablets
5 gallons - 20 tablets

- Drop tablet(s) into container and screw cap on loosely.
- Wait 5 minutes, then shake container to wet screw threads.
- Wait another 35 minutes before drinking the water.
- To eliminate iodine taste, wait 20 minutes after iodine treatment, then add I neutralizing tablet for every iodine tablet used.
- For muddy water, first strain the water through a cloth or T shirt to remove dirt particles, then treat.

Note: This method is used by members of the military and the Peace Corps. Next to boiling, it's the safest way to treat small quantities water.

Solar Method

- Put water in a clear glass jar, clear water bottle, or clear jug.
- Leave it in the sun for about 6 hours.

Note: This method is recommended by the World Health Organization. It uses the sun's UV rays to disinfect water and kills 99% of all bacteria. It's the cheapest and simplest, but slowest, methods of water purification.

ALTERNATE WATER SOURCES INSIDE YOUR HOME

Water heater. Depending on its size, your water heater contains 25 to 50 gallons of drinkable water. To drain water from your water heater, first make sure your electricity or gas is shut off, then turn on a hot-water faucet to provide air flow in the line. Put a pan under the cleanout drain at the bottom of the tank, attach a hose to the cleanout drain, open the drain valve, and pour the water into a container.

Note: If you have an electric water heater make sure you fill your tank before turning on your electricity or you will burn out your heating elements.

Bathtub. A bathtub can hold 35 to 50 gallons of water. We purchased a plastic water bladder, called an AquaPod, that fits inside our bathtub and holds up to 70 gallons. It keeps the water clean, and helps keep the water from evaporating.

Plumbing system. You may have many gallons of water trapped in the water lines of your plumbing system. To drain your system, first turn on a faucet at the highest point of you plumbing system to provide air flow, then turn on a faucet at the lowest point to drain the water remaining in the lines.

Toilet. Your toilet tank will contain 2 to 5 gallons of water depending on the type of toilet. Take the lid off the toilet tank to scoop water out with a cup or pitcher. Make sure you treat it before drinking it.

Waterbed. A king-size water bed will contain 150 to 250 gallons of water. However, when you filled your water bed you probably used a copper sulphate algicide to treat the water. Copper sulphate is toxic, but can be removed by treating the water in your waterbed with a water filter.

ALTERNATE WATER SOURCES OUTSIDE YOUR HOME

Swimming pool. The high doses of chlorine and other chemicals normally used in pools can be toxic. Too much chlorine (greater than 4 ppm) is not recommended for drinking). 3 ppm or less, is okay. You can easily test this with chlorine test strips.

We recommend using pool water for washing and cleaning.

Ponds, streams, lakes, and rivers. Unless you're absolutely sure an outdoor water source is safe, filter, boil, or treat that water. Water weighs 8 pounds per gallon, so if you're carrying water long distances, use small jugs or water bags.

Rainwater. Rainwater is nature's purest form of water, but if you live where there's a lot of air pollution, or if you collect it from your roof, it's best to treat it. Collect rainwater from your roof by running your downspout into a water barrel or clean garbage can. You can also collect rainwater by covering a hole dug in the ground with a large plastic sheet.

Snow. In winter, many parts of the country will have an abundance of snow. To turn snow into water, melt it in a pot on a stove.

Avoid eating too much snow. Doing so will lower your body temperature and will cause you to dehydrate.

How Much Water to Store

You need 2 to 2-1/2 quarts of water per day just to survive. That amount doesn't include water for cooking, bathing, washing clothes, and washing dishes.

Using the water recycling system I'll talk about in Chapter 4, you can drink, eat, bathe, and wash your dishes with just 1 gallon of water per day. Multiply that times 30 days, and you'll need to store 30 gallons of water per person, per month.

A 1-month supply of water is the rock-bottom minimum I'd recommend anyone store. If you have the means and the storage room, I recommend storing 2-3 months' worth. Better to be safe than sorry, especially with something you literally can't live without.

Grace and I store our water in 7-gallon jugs we bought at our local discount store for $10 each, and a 55-gallon water barrel we bought online. We treat our water using the bleach method above, and store 1 months' worth (10 containers total) in our garage and in various places around our house.

We have 45 gallons of drinking water in our hot water heater, 10 gallons in our toilets, and will fill our guest bathtub with 50 gallons of water as things start getting worse. That will give us a total of 230 gallons of water, or a four-month supply for the two of us.

In addition to drinking water, we also store water in two 35-gallon trash cans for washing and cleaning.

We have a water filter that cost us $30, which we'll use if we need to get water from outside sources (puddles, ponds, or our local river). Our filter is good for about 500 gallons, giving us an additional 8 months' worth of drinking water.

FREQUENTLY ASKED QUESTIONS

What about storing bottled water?

Good idea if you don't have the time to treat and store your own water. However, it can get expensive if you use bottled water for washing and cleaning.

How long will treated water last?

If you take proper precautions in sealing and storing your water so that bacteria or other contaminants don't get into it, your water could stay good indefinitely. But because bacteria, viruses and other microbes may survive and multiply, it's a good idea to retreat or replace your water every year.

Where do I get products to treat water?

You can get unscented bleach (Clorox or generic brands) at your local supermarket or discount store. Iodine tablets, such as Potable Aqua, and water filters can be purchased at your local sporting goods store, discount store, or online.

I live in a one-bedroom condominium with limited space. Where can I store water?

If you're pressed for storage space, think small. Put your water in smaller containers - cleaned soda and juice bottles, 1-to-2-gallon jugs - and store them anywhere you can - under sinks, on spare shelves, under your bed, and wherever else you can think of. Do not use milk jugs as they are made to degrade and will leak over time.

When things start getting worse, fill your bathtubs, sinks, extra pots, and any other containers you have with water. Bathtubs hold about 30 to 50 gallons of water and sinks hold 3 to 6 gallons.

RECOMMENDED RESOURCES

Visit **www.frugalsurvivalist.com** for information about the products listed below or to purchase them:

Water containers and water pump

Water Bob

Water filters

WATER CONTAINERS AND WATER TREATMENT SUPPLIES

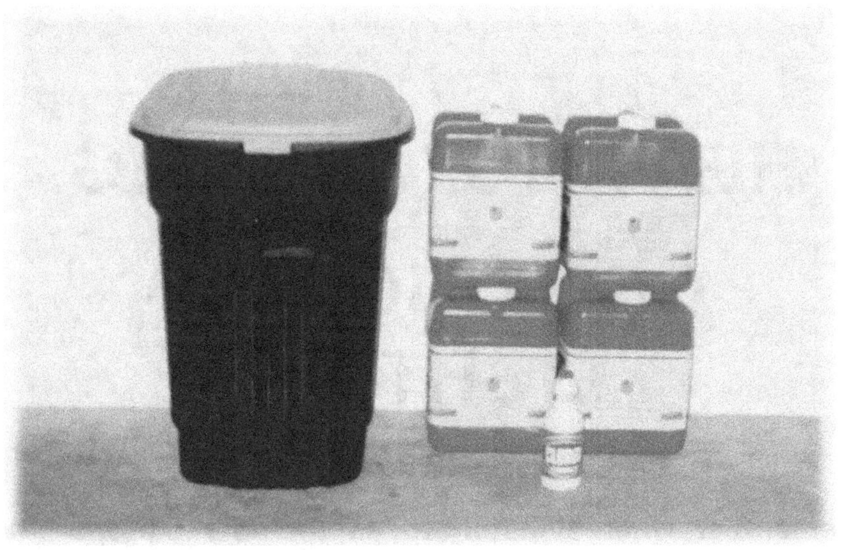

Water jugs for holding drinking water, plastic trash can for holding washing water, and chlorine bleach to treat the water.

- 3 -

HEATING, COOLING, COOKING, AND LIGHTING

"Remember, when disaster strikes, the time to prepare has passed."

- Steven Cyros

Imagine for a moment that all the power in your home is out.

Now think about what you'd want to have.

First, if it's winter, you'll probably want a source of heat. If its summer, you'll want something to cool you down.

Next, you'll undoubtedly want some light. You'll also want a stove to cook your food, and a radio so you can listen to the Emergency Broadcasting System, or your local radio station, to find out what's going on.

If the power goes down, and you are one of those people who thought it just couldn't happen here, you'll be sitting in the dark wishing you had any or all of the above-mentioned items.

If, on the other hand, you are one of those people who decided that a little preparation was in order, you've flipped on your flashlight to look for your kerosene lantern and your battery-operated radio. If it's winter, your fireplace or propane heater is ready to go so all you have to do is light it and wait for the warmth to come flooding into your living room. And if it's summer, you've stripped down to your bare essentials and turned on your battery-operated fan to keep you cool.

As you sit on your couch, reading one of your favorite books by the light of a kerosene lamp while listening to your favorite music on your battery powered radio or MP3 player, you're drinking some hot chocolate, coffee, or hot buttered rum you heated up on your gas stove. Ah, the joys of being prepared.

HEATING

If a snowstorm, hurricane, or tornado knocks down your electric power lines, you could be without power for weeks on end. If your electric or gas company goes belly up, you could be without electricity or gas for months. Even if you use propane gas from an outside tank, loss of electricity will incapacitate your blower fan and your thermostat.

We hardly think about electricity or gas until it goes out. Only then do we realize how dependent on it we are. During the recent La Nina-generated snowstorms, thousands of people were caught off guard and had to be evacuated to shelters because they didn't have back up heating, cooking, or lighting.

If you live in the sunbelt, you won't have air conditioning or be able to use fans if your electricity goes out.

Grace and I live in the high desert of Arizona where the temperatures occasionally drop below freezing. If the heat goes out in winter, we'll move our bed and our winter clothes into the living room, and close off the rest of the house.

For added warmth we'll put our guestroom mattresses in an upright position against the back of our couch to form a reflector between us and our propane heater.

We'll wear long underwear beneath our sweaters and jeans, and if it really gets cold, we'll wear our down-filled jackets inside the house.

Propane Heaters

We recently purchased a propane heater for $30. These heaters give of an amazing amount of heat - 15,000 BTUs - the equivalent of 15 space heaters. Our heater mounts directly to a standard 20-pound propane tank, and features a variable heat control valve so we can set it for a temperature that's right for us.

This heater is easy to start, requires no electricity, has a high efficiency heat reflector, and comes with a safety shutoff.

Propane heaters range in price from $30 for a 15,000 BTU model, to $70 for a two burner, 30,000 BTU model which is adequate for heating one or two rooms.

Wood Stoves and Fireplaces

Most fireplaces in homes today were built more for effect than for heat. If you have a built-in fireplace, odds are it won't heat your house. Why? Because these types of fireplaces draw the warm air from inside your home to feed the fire, then shoot it up the chimney along with most of the heat from the fire.

If you have a built-in fireplace you have two options: I) you can buy an insert that will make your fireplace infinitely more efficient, 2) you can buy a heat exchanger, a series of "C" shaped tubes welded together, that will also increase efficiency.

If you can't afford either of these devices, use your damper to prevent heat from going up the chimney. Open it up just enough to allow smoke to rise in the chimney and prevent heat from rising with it.

If you have a free-standing wood stove, you're in luck. Even small airtight stoves will heat large areas. They have the added benefit of your being able to cook on them.

If you use a wood stove or fireplace, I recommend buying hardwood as it will give you more heat for your money. Plus, it burns longer than softwood so you don't have to restock your fireplace as often.

In some areas you can get free wood from public parklands, forests, dumps, constructions sites, and lumber mills. Make sure to get dry wood or allow it to dry out for a couple of months before burning it.

An alternative to wood logs is to tightly roll up newspapers into logs, then tie them with string. Not the greatest, but newspaper logs do work in a pinch.

Dress Warmly

The first rule of staying warm is to dress warn. I've camped out at 45 degrees below zero in Alaska and stayed warm because I knew how to dress for the weather. The secret is layering - putting on layers of clothing to trap enough air to insulate you from the cold.

Another secret is to wear a hat. Because heat rises, much of your body heat is lost through your head.

If you live in a cold climate, make sure you have the following:

- Thermal underwear and heavy socks to wear underneath your clothes.
- Hats, gloves, and winter coats.
- Plenty of blankets, comforters, or sleeping bags for every member of your family

If you live in really cold climates like Canada, Minnesota, North Dakota, or Alaska, you might want to include:

- Insulated hats, vests, insulated boots, and synthetic or down filled jackets and pants.

In a pinch, crumpled up newspapers or plastic bags stuffed between layers of clothing, or stuffed between your blanket and sheets, provides an amazing amount of insulation.

COOLING

If you live in the sun belt, you won't have air-conditioning or be able to use fans if the electricity goes out.

Grace and I have two battery operated fans that we purchased for $18 each. They're quiet, easy to use, and produce an amazing amount of air flow for their size. If you set these fans on low, they'll run for about two weeks at 2 to 3 hours a day before you have to replace or recharge your batteries. For night use, they'll run for up to four days.

Another way to keep cool is to set up your living quarters in the coolest part of your house. Basements and rooms on the north side of the house are usually the coolest.

If your house really heats up, and you don't have a porch, consider rigging a tent, tarp, or some sheets on the north side of your house for shade. In Arizona, pioneers used to work outside under their porches during the day, and sleep under them at night.

If you live in an area where the nights are cool, like we do, use the thermos bottle principle to capture the cool night air. Open all your windows at night to let in the cool air, then close them in the morning to keep it in. To help keep the sun's heat from entering your house, cover the inside of your windows with tin foil or light-colored sheets.

Dress Cool

To stay cool, dress cool. Wear the bare minimum of light-weight clothing. Clothes should be loose-fitting and light-colored to reflect the sun's rays. A hat or umbrella is another good way to reflect sunshine.

Limit strenuous physical activity to the cool hours of the morning and evening. Keep physical activity to a minimum during the day and stay indoors or in the shade.

Drink lots of water so your body will have enough to cool you off through perspiration. If you have extra water and live in a dry climate, fill a spray bottle with water and spray yourself occasionally to cool down.

COOKING

Gas Stoves

My personal choice for a dependable stove is the good ol' Coleman propane stove. I've used Coleman stoves off and on for more than 30 years, and I can't say enough about the reliability and versatility of these stoves. I've seen these stoves boiling up moose stew in Alaska, merrily hissing away while heating tea at a glacier lake in Canada, and cooking up turtle soup on the beach of a remote Caribbean island.

Coleman makes 3 types of stoves - propane, butane, and gas.

Propane stove: I like their propane stove because it's easier to use than the gas models, it's less expensive than white gas or butane when you use the larger 20-and 30-pound propane tanks, and is less flammable than gas. Plus, propane has an indefinite shelf life, while gas does not.

The main drawback to propane is that it won't work in temperatures below 0° F.

To operate a propane stove, you simply attach the tank to the stove, turn on the valve, and light it up.

Propane stoves can be purchased at camping stores, discount stores, and online. They cost about $60 for a two-burner model.

Pros
Least expensive
Easy to operate
Fuel has indefinite shelf life
Burns clean
Very little odor
Has windscreen for outdoor use

Cons
Does not work below 0 degrees

White gas stove: White gas burns a little hotter and cleaner than regular gas, and is less likely to clog the stove's generator than regular gas. White gas will last 5 to 7 years in its container if unopened, and about 2 years after it's opened.

White gas is much more expensive than either propane or regular gas, coming in at $13 dollars a gallon.

To operate a gas stove, you pour fuel into the tank, pressurize it by pumping, turn on the gas, then light the burner. The flame bums hot and will boil a quart of water in 4 minutes or less.

You can purchase gas stoves at discount stores, sporting goods stores, or online. A two-burner model costs about $60. Coleman makes an oven which you can use to make bread, rolls, cakes, and even small pizzas. It costs $35.

If you buy a gas stove, I recommend you buy an extra generator. In the unlikely event you have a problem with one of these stoves it will probably be the generator that goes out. Generators usually last an average of 400 hours using white gas.

Pros
Inexpensive
Fuel burns hot
Burns clean
Very little odor
Has windscreen for outdoor use

Cons
Fuel is expensive
Fuel is very flammable
Fuel has limited shelf life

Regular Gas Stove: These stoves are similar to white gas stoves, with the exception that you can burn both white gas and regular gas in it, which currently, is the cheapest type of fuel.

Unfortunately, these stoves aren't cheap, costing around $120. Additionally, the stove's generator has a tendency to clog up, so you'll need to buy an extra generator or two.

Pros
Fuel is cheap
Uses regular gasoline
Fuel burns hot
Very little odor
Has windscreen for outdoor use

Cons
Stoves are expensive
Fuel is very flammable
Fuel has a one-year shelf life

Kerosene Stoves

One of the best meals I've ever eaten - swordfish steaks with creole-style vegetables - was cooked on a remote Caribbean island with a vintage, 50-year-old kerosene stove. The smell of that stove was awful, but the food it cooked was wonderful.

The main virtue of kerosene stoves is their simplicity. Like a kerosene lamp, a kerosene stove is just a container holding an adjustable wick. You light the wick and adjust it up or down for temperature control. The drawback to these stoves is the odor they give off, and the soot that can coat your walls if you don't use top-grade (I -K) kerosene.

Kerosene stoves are hard to find, but can be ordered through camping and boating catalogs, and online. Prices range from $20 to $50.

Pros
Inexpensive
Simple to operate
Simple design
Fuel is least flammable

Cons
Top grade kerosene is expensive
Gives of a strong kerosene odor

Alcohol Stove

The simplest and cheapest stove of all. These stoves are the darlings of ultralight backpackers and boating enthusiasts. You can get one of these stoves for less than $10.

To operate these stoves all you do is fill the stove with alcohol, take of the top, and light it. Some stoves have temperature regulators, and some do not. Fuel costs about $25 a gallon.

Pros
Cheap
Simple to operate
Simple design
Very little odor
Fuel shelf life is indefinite

Cons
Fuel is expensive
Fuel is very flammable

Solar Cooker

I love our solar cooker. We can cook anything in it and it requires no fuel at all. These cookers will cook your food on a cloudy day and even in winter.

A few years ago I attended a solar fair here in my home town. One of the most interesting things I saw there was a group of about 20 people sitting around in a circle cooking various foods on a variety of home-made solar ovens. What amazed me was these people were cooking everything from meat loaf, to bread, to a chocolate cake in ovens that required no fuel ... and they were doing it on an overcast day in the middle of winter!

Solar ovens are safe, they'll cook virtually anything, they require no fuel, and they have no moving parts to wear out. Solar ovens will reach temperatures of 400º F, and can be used in below 0 temperatures (a solar oven was used on Mt. Everest).

They are a little on the pricey side - ours cost $79 - but when you consider the fact that these cookers use no fuel, they are a bargain at any price, especially during a financial crisis when fuel may be in limited supply, or unavailable. If you can't afford one, you can find plans for them online, and you can make one for as little as $5.

To use a solar cooker all you do is take it outside, point it toward the sun, put your pot with food in it inside the cooker, and wait.

Pros
Uses no fuel
Simple to operate
Easy to make yourself

Cons
Longest cooking time
Does not work on really overcast or rainy days
Must be used outside

LIGHTING

Flashlights (battery operated)

Flashlights are your first line of defense for any power outages at night. I recommend keeping one beside your bed, and a couple more stashed in convenient locations around your house.

Flashlights range in size from key-chain lights, to monster boating lights that can light up a football field.

My favorite flashlight is an LED mini light. This wonder of modern ingenuity is about the size of a roll of Lifesavers, yet gives off enough light to allow me to see on the darkest of nights. It's rugged, reliable, and water resistant.

I keep a mini light on my bedside dresser. I have another one in the glove compartment of my car, one in a drawer in the kitchen, and one in our garage. At $10 for six of them, these flashlights are worth their weight in gold.

We also have 2 LED lanterns we purchased for $18 that we'll use for reading, eating, and playing games at night, and 2 kerosene lanterns.

If you feel you need a lot of light, you can get an LED lantern for around $12 that will light up the whole neighborhood.

Flashlights (hand crank)

Hand crank flashlights are great because they don't require batteries, but they will also give you a good case of hand cramps if used for any length of time. With older models you had to continuously crank the flashlight to get any light. Newer models give you an average of eight minutes to one hour of light, depending on the model, for every minute you crank them.

These flashlights cost anywhere from $10 to $20. The model we like is a combination hand crank and solar powered flashlight we got for $10 on Amazon.

Solar Battery Charger

Grace and I have a small solar charger that will charge most sizes of batteries from AAA's to the larger D sizes. We use our charger to recharge batteries for our flashlights, radio, portable stereo, remotes, wireless mouse, and clock batteries. Our charger does take a long time to charge batteries, so we just load it with batteries in the morning, place it in the sun, and take out the batteries at night.

Our charger cost us $45, and it, too, will be worth its weight in gold if the financial crisis lasts for any length of time. Rechargeable Ni-MH batteries cost $2 to $5 apiece depending on the size, but they'll last a lifetime. Considering the number of times most people replace regular batteries, rechargeable batteries end up costing much less over time.

If you can't afford a solar charger, make sure you have enough fresh batteries for all your flashlights and at least one small radio. I recommend buying alkaline batteries as opposed to carbon-zinc (heavy-duty) batteries. Alkaline batteries, though slightly more expensive than carbon-zinc batteries, outlast them by 2 to 3 times. Alkaline batteries have a shelf life of 10 years when stored at room temperature.

Candles

Candles have been mankind's source of light for hundreds of years. They're simple, foolproof, and available everywhere. Unfortunately, they don't give off much light, and most of them don't last very long.

I've used candles in a variety of situations, from reading comic books in the outhouse as a Boy Scout, to almost setting my house on fire when I blew out the 52 candles on my last birthday cake. I like candles, but in a survival situation I'd much rather have a kerosene lamp or battery-operated lantern because they give off much more light.

One overlooked drawback to candles is they can be dangerous. Every year there are numerous incidents of candles setting houses on fire, especially during the holidays. Unattended candles can fall over, or melt down, igniting whatever they're-sitting on.

If you use candles, make sure you keep them in a candle holder, preferably with a glass globe, and never leave a burning candle unattended.

Specialty candles that come in a tin container and burn for 100 hours can be purchased online.

Kerosene Lamps

I've always loved the glow of a kerosene lamp. Its warm yellow flame dances in the dark, casting shadows on walls, and seems to have a life of its own.

I lived for 6 years with kerosene lighting in Oregon and Alaska, and I discovered that once your eyes get used to low-level lighting, you can see almost as well as you can with electric lights. The myth that dim lighting causes you to go blind is just that - a myth.

Another advantage to using low-level lighting in survival conditions is when you go outside at night your eyes are partially accustomed to the dark. You'll see much better than you would coming from a brightly lit environment.

Kerosene lamps are dependable, simple to operate, and inexpensive to buy. When you first light a kerosene lantern you turn up the wick until it begins to smoke, then turn it down until it stops. Keeping the wick turned down below the smoking point prevents soot build-up on the lantern's glass chimney. To extinguish a kerosene lamp, just blow downward across the top of the chimney.

The only maintenance you need to do is occasionally trim the wick. When you notice carbon build up on the wick or it looks a little ragged, cut it straight and level with a pair of scissors.

You can purchase kerosene lamps from your local discount store, hardware store, sporting goods store, or online. They cost anywhere from $12 to $20, and come in a variety of shapes and sizes.

I recommend buying at least one glass-bottom kerosene lamp (that lets you see how much fuel you have left) and one outdoor hurricane lantern (the kind with a metal top and carrying handle). Buying an extra chimney and set of wicks is also a good idea.

Kerosene can be purchased where you buy your lantern, or in bulk containers at gas stations and hardware stores. It has a shelf life of 10 years.

Aladdin Lamps

Aladdin lamps are a variation on kerosene lamps. They use a mantle-type wick for maximum surface area to give off maximum light. These lamps give off about the same amount of light as a 60-watt bulb, and burn extremely hot. If you use one of these lanterns be careful. I almost burned a hole in the roof of my cabin in Alaska with an Aladdin lamp due to the heat that shoots up its glass chimney.

Aladdin lamps can be purchased at some hardware stores, emergency supply stores, and online. They cost about $170.

Gas Lanterns

If you want a lot of light, say the equivalent of a 75-watt bulb, then gas lanterns are the way to go. Personally, I don't care for them because they make noise, they give off a glaring light, and their wicks (mantles as they're called) are fragile.

When you first light a new gas lantern its sack-like mantle immediately turns to ash. It's not a mistake, that's what's supposed to happen. Somehow these lanterns work with an ash wick, and that's why they're so fragile. They burn for 8 hours on high, per tank of fuel, and up to 14 hours on a low.

Another drawback to using these babies is they use a lot of gas and they bum hotter than the hellfires. I've seen a number of first-time users grab the wire handle of one of these lamps only to end up yelping and dancing around camp shaking a singed hand in utter agony. Use a pot holder on the handle when hot.

Coleman dual fuel lanterns cost $80, and can be purchased at discount stores, sporting goods stores, and online.

Propane Lanterns

Propane lamps seem to be the coming thing in camping. They're easy to use and give off almost as much light as gas lanterns

The drawbacks to these lamps are they're expensive to operate when used with small containers, and because they use the same type of mantle as gas lamps, they're fragile. For extended use you can buy an adapter to attach the lantern to a larger propane tank making it much more economical.

Propane gas has and indefinite shelf life, and you can buy propane lanterns at the same places you buy gas lanterns.

Matches and Lighters

A box of safety matches contains 300 matches and costs $2. A Bic lighter will give you over 2,000 lights and costs $1. I recommend having at least one of each to light your fireplace, heater, lamps, and stove. Grace and I keep 4 lighters and 2 boxes of safety matches in a kitchen drawer.

Fuel Storage and Fire Safety

- Store all fuels in approved containers, in a ventilated area away from ignition sources, and excessive heat.
- Store fuel away from food so food will not absorb odor.
- Store matches and lighters where children cannot reach them.
- Make sure your chimney is clean before using your fireplace to prevent chimney fires.
- Read directions carefully before operating any fuel-operated device.
- When using heaters, stoves, or lanterns, always open a window for ventilation to prevent carbon monoxide poisoning.
- Fill all fuel-operated devices outside your home.
- Always have an ABC-type fire extinguisher handy when you use heaters, stoves, or lanterns.

- Keep all fuel-operated devices a safe distance from flammable objects.
- Never leave burning heaters, stoves, or lanterns unattended.
- Turn off heaters and lanterns before going to bed.
- Use battery operated smoke detectors, and check your batteries once a year.

FREQUENTLY ASKED QUESTIONS

How about getting a gas-powered generator to run the appliances in my home?

Unless you need a generator to run medical equipment or to run a pump for well water, I don't recommend buying a generator. Not only are they expensive to buy, they are expensive to run. Also, gasoline breaks down after about 6 months, and is highly flammable.

That being said, if you can afford one, afford the gas to operate it, and can put up with the noise and smell, I'd say go for it.

I've lived for a number of years in a variety of locations without electricity and I can't think of a time when I needed a gas generator.

Why not get some solar panels?

Solar panels are an ideal way to generate power. They're virtually maintenance free and require nothing but the sun to generate electricity. However, buying enough photovoltaic panels to run all the appliances, lights, and air conditioner in your home would cost $10,000 to $25,000.

If you have the money to install solar panels, it's well worth the initial expense and will save you thousands of dollars on your electric bill down the road.

If you don't have the money, an inexpensive solar battery charger, similar to the one Grace and I have, will charge batteries to run flashlights, electric lanterns, radios, clocks, small fans, portable stereos, and other battery-operated appliances. For $20 we even have a solar charger that will charge our cell phones, tablets, and MP3 players.

How about using my gas barbecue for cooking?

You can use your barbecue, but because the burners don't concentrate heat like stove burners do, it's not very efficient. You'd be better off buying a propane stove, and an adapter to use that stove with your barbecue's propane tank.

RECOMMENDED RESOURCES

Visit **www.frugalsurvivalist.com** for information about the products listed below or to purchase them:

Flash lights

Kerosene lamps and accessories

Gas stoves and ovens

Solar ovens
Propane

Propane tank

Battery operated fan

Rechargeable batteries

Cooling towels

Misting stand

Evaporative cooling hat

HEATING, COOKING, AND LIGHTING SUPPLIES

A fireplace, camp stove and fuel, two types of kerosene lanterns, kerosene lamp oil, and flashlights.

- 4 -

HYGIENE

"Take care of your body. It's the only place you have to live."

- Jim Rohn

Your health is your greatest possession, and good hygiene is the key to good health, especially under emergency conditions.

Things we take for granted now - a constant flow of water to keep ourselves clean, regular garbage collection, sewage disposal - could all be jeopardized by the financial crisis.

How do you keep your body clean and free of bacteria with a minimal amount of water? What do you do with germ-infested garbage without garbage collection? How do you get rid of human waste without polluting and possibly infecting your neighborhood?

Oftentimes more people die of the diseases that follow a catastrophe, due to unsanitary conditions, than they do in the catastrophe itself. Good hygiene and sanitation are critical to your survival.

BATHING, DISH WASHING, AND LAUNDRY

Thirty years ago I read a book, *The Enchanted Vagabonds*, that changed my life. It was the inspiration for my traveling and living in Alaska, Canada, and the Caribbean.

The book tells the story of Dana and Ginger Lamb, a young couple who, during the Great Depression, decided to journey from California to Central America in a home-made kayak. One of the chapters explained how they prepared for their trip, and how they taught themselves to conserve water in order to survive the desert conditions of Mexico. They discovered that using a washcloth they could wash themselves with just 1 cup of water and get themselves perfectly clean. It's amazing what you can do with a little ingenuity.

Grace and I use a system similar to the Lambs (we've added a few more cups of water), and also recycle our bath water, dishwater, and clothes-washing water to flush our toilet. I used this method for 6 years in Alaska. It's simple and it works like a champ.

With this system you need only 1 gallon of water per person per day to bathe, do your dishes, wash your clothes, and flush your toilet. Heres' how:

WASH-WATER RECYCLNG SYSTEM

Bathing

- Fill a pot with 1 quart of water and warm it on your stove.
- Place a large washtub or plastic storage tub near the stove to stand in.
- Using a cup as a dipper, slowly pour 1 cup of water into your hair, rubbing it in with your other hand, then shampoo.
- Strip off excess soap suds from your hair with your hands and shake them into the washtub, then slowly pour another cup of water on your hair to rinse it.

- When your hair is rinsed, slowly pour the next cup of water over your body, rubbing it over your skin with your free hand.
- Soap up and wash yourself using a washcloth, then wipe off any excess soap, wringing it into the washtub
- Pour the last cup of water over your body, using your free hand to rinse yourself clean.
- Towel yourself dry, and save the used wash water in a bucket to use to flush your toilet.

Note: You can save fuel by using a solar shower to heat your water. Solar showers are heavy-duty plastic bags that you fill with water then lay in the sun for a couple of hours. These showers have a temperature gauge so you don't overheat your water, and a shower head that makes rinsing off quick and easy.

I've used one of these wonderful contraptions a number of times when I've gone camping and I wouldn't leave home without one. They can't be beat for quick, convenient, fuel-free showers. Solar showers range in size from 3-quart single-size showers, to 5-gallon family-size showers, to a 10-gallon maxi showers. Prices start at $12.

Solar showers can be purchased at discount stores, sporting goods stores, and online.

Dish washing

- Place dishes in your sink or a dishpan filled with water and detergent and soak them.
- Wash dishes, using a course-sided sponge, stacking dishes to one side or putting them in a dish rack.
- Pour used dishwater into the bucket you use to store toilet water.
- Pour hot water into dishpan, and rinse dishes, leaving the used water in the pan to soak the next day's dishes.

Note: You can buy dishpans at discount and dollar stores for $1 to $2.

Clothes Washing

- Pretreat stains by rubbing a small amount of detergent, or an appropriate stain remover, into clothes. Rub the fabric back and forth against itself, using the knuckles of your hands, to remove the stain.
- Soak your clothing for half an hour in a tub filled with enough soapy to just cover them.
- Take a clean toilet plunger and move it up and down in the tub to agitate the water and clean your clothes.
- Pour used wash water into your toilet-water bucket.
- Wring your clothes over your toilet-water bucket by twisting them.
- Put your clothes back into tub, pour in warm water and soak clothes for a couple of minutes to loosen detergent.
- Plunge your clothes with your plunger to remove the detergent, then remove your clothes and wring over your toilet-water bucket. Save the rinse water to wash the next batch of clothes.
- Dry clothing outdoors on a clothesline.

Note: The only clothes you need to change daily are your underwear. If you wear underpants, panties, and undershirts underneath your regular clothes, you will only need to wash your shirts, pants, and other outer clothes once a week That way you conserve water.

If you don't have an area outside where you can put up a clothesline, you can dry your clothes by hanging them on lines strung inside your shower.

Toilet Flushing

To minimize water use, flush your toilet only once a day (twice if you have a large family) using recycled waste water.

- After using your toilet, cover the bowl with saran wrap or plastic sheeting to minimize odor. Keep the bathroom window open and the bathroom door shut.
- To flush your toilet, pour recycled wash water into the toilet tank and flush.

Note: To neutralize odor you can add camp-toilet deodorizer, a teaspoon or two of bleach, or a little Lysol to your toilet bowl.

Toilet Bucket Method

This is the new and revised method that European noblemen and women used in the 17th and 18th centuries to remove their bowel movements. They used what they called a chamber pot.

- Line a 5-gallon bucket with a 13-gallon garbage bag.
- Unscrew your toilet seat from your toilet and place it on top of the bucket.
- After you go to the bathroom, pour a little bit of bleach or Pinesol into the bucket to help contain the odor
- After a few days, tie the bag and either bury it outside, or place it outside away from your house to take to the dump or have your garbage man pick it up when garbage collection resumes.

Note: You can purchase a toilet bucket with a lid and seat for around $40, and compostable liners for $10.

Composting Toilet Method

- Feces can be safely returned to the soil by digging a large hole in the ground.
- Use a camp toilet or plastic bucket to relieve yourself.
- Empty the camp toilet or bucket into the toilet hole each morning.
- Cover the feces with a layer of dirt to keep flies away, then cover the hole with a piece of plywood or a garbage can top with a rock on it to keep out four-legged pests.
- Rinse your bucket with used wash water after using it.

- Note: When you bury feces they are eventually rendered harmless by aerobic decomposition. Decomposition may be sped up by sprinkling lime over the fecal matter.

Waterless Washing Method

If you have absolutely no room to store water for washing yourself or your dishes, you can use baby wipes to wash yourself and paper or Styrofoam plates and bowls to eat with.

A 4-month supply of baby wipes for two people (240 wipes) is about the size of a small box of cereal and costs less than $5. Use them to clean your underarms, private areas, and body parts that are dirty. You can also clean your hair with them.

We have a supply of 300 Styrofoam bowls that cost us $6. If we need to conserve water, those bowls will last us 2 months.

If need be you can use one spoon for all your meals and clean it with a wipe.

If you use one pot to cook in every day, you can wipe it clean with paper towels. Heating it up when you cook in it will destroy harmful bacteria. To dispose of the plates and wipes, simply burn them or bury them.

Garbage Disposal

Reduce garbage to minimum size by squashing all boxes, cans, and plastic bottles. If the lack of garbage collection is only temporary, keep your garbage in your garage or in garbage cans with lids on them to prevent animals from rummaging through it.

If there's no garbage collection for a long period of time, burn flammable garbage, or use it as fire starter, and bury everything else until you can recycle it at a later date.

FREQUENTLY ASKED QUESTIONS

I live in an apartment building. What can I do about sewage disposal?

Get your landlord to lease a portable toilet, the kind you see at construction sites. If he won't do it, see if you can round up some of your neighbors to help spread out the cost.

RECOMMENDED RESOURCES

Visit **www.frugalsurvivalist.com** for information about the products listed below or to purchase them:

Clothes line and clothes pins
Clothes washing plunger
Dish washing tub
Bathing tub
Portable toilet
Solar shower

WASHTUB, PORTABLE TOILET, DISHPAN, CLOTHESLINE

A washtub for bathing, a portable toilet, plastic dishpan
for washing dishes, and clothes pins and clothesline.

- 5 -

First Aid

"Never say 'That won't happen to me.' Life has a funny way of proving us wrong."

- Unknown

What would happen if you had a medical emergency and couldn't get help? What would you do if your spouse suddenly became unconscious, or your child lacerated his hand with a knife, and you couldn't get to a doctor?

Knowing what to do in a medical emergency can mean the difference between life and death, for you or someone you love.

Before I made my journey to Alaska, I took every first aid course that was available, and read everything I could find on handling medical emergencies. When you're out in the bush, miles from civilization and medical help, your life depends on knowing how to take care of yourself.

The same holds true if you have a medical emergency and you can't call an ambulance or a doctor for help.

If you haven't already done so, I strongly urge you and your family members to take a first aid course and a course in CPR (Cardiopulmonary Resuscitation). These courses cost only a few dollars and will take just a few hours of your time. I would also urge you to purchase a good book on first aid to use as a reference.

The following are basic first-aid instructions:

- **Remain calm.**
- **If it's a life-threatening emergency, call or have someone call 911 for medical help immediately. Check the victim's ABC's - Airway (open victim's airway by tilting her head back and lifting her chin), Breathing (look at his chest and put your ear to his mouth to listen for signs of breathing), Circulation (check for a pulse by placing 73**

- **your index (first finger) and middle fingers on their wrist, at the base of their thumb).**
- **If the victim is not breathing or has no pulse, immediately begin CPR.**
- **Treat the victim first for bleeding (use latex gloves to avoid infection), then burns, then broken bones and shock.**
- **DO NOT move the victim unless absolutely necessary.**

Amputation (body part torn or cut from body)

- Stop the bleeding and treat the victim for shock (see Bleeding and Shock below).
- If you cannot stop the bleeding with arterial pressure, use a tourniquet as a last resort. Wrap a gauze bandage, tie, or length of cloth above the amputation and tie it with a half knot. Place a spoon, screwdriver, stick or similar object on top of the knot, then tie it again. Twist the spoon to tighten the tourniquet until the flow of blood stops, then tie the spoon, stick, or screwdriver in place.
- Check for breathing and pulse and begin CPR if necessary (see CPR below).
- Wrap the detached body part in clean cloth or put it in a plastic bag to be sent with victim to hospital. If available,

put the wrapped body part in bag or container with ice to keep it cool. Do not freeze the body part or allow it to touch the ice.

- Seek immediate medical help.

Animal Bite (pain, bleeding, tingling sensation)

- Clean the bitten area with soap and water or an antiseptic wipe, then bandage it.
- Seek medical help if the animal was wild, was not immunized against rabies, or if you experience intermittent rage, seizures, or paralysis after the incident.

Appendicitis (sharp pain in lower right abdomen, nausea, fever)

- Have the victim lie down. If available, put ice on the affected area to alleviate pain.
- Make sure the victim does not eat or drink.
- Seek medical help immediately.

Bleeding (flowing or spurting blood)

- Have the victim lie on his back and, if there are no fractures, elevate the wound above his heart. Quickly remove foreign objects from the wound.

- Check for breathing and pulse and apply CPR if necessary (see CPR below).

- Apply firm steady pressure to the wound with gauze pad, clean cloth, or your hand to stop the bleeding. Keep pressure on the wound for at least 10 minutes before checking to see if the bleeding has stopped.

- If the bleeding does not stop, maintain pressure on the wound and apply firm pressure to the artery between the wound and the heart with your other hand. **For arms and hands**, squeeze the artery on the inner side of the upper arm against the bone. **For legs and feet**, press against the inner thigh near the groin with the heel of your hand. Do not apply pressure to the arteries leading to the head or neck unless bright red blood is spurting from neck.

- Bandage the wound after the bleeding stops (bandage over the original bandage or cloth).

- If the victim is bleeding internally, keep him still. If his arm or leg is swollen, immobilize it and treat him for shock (see Shock below).

- Seek medical help if the wound is severe or the bleeding is internal.

Breathing Stopped (unconsciousness, bluish skin color)

- Call 911 or have someone else call.

- Immediately begin CPR (see CPR below).
- Continue until the victim revives or medical help arrives.

Broken (Fractured) Bones and Dislocations (pain, swelling, deformity, exposed bone)

- Do not move the victim.
- Check for breathing and pulse, and give CPR if necessary (see CPR below).
- Treat for bleeding (see Bleeding).
- Splint the arm or leg in the position it is found. Do not try to straighten the limb or try to push the bone back through the skin.
- **Finger or toe**. If a finger or toe is broken, apply a cool, water-soaked cloth to injured area and elevate it above the heart. Put a finger splint or rolled cardboard on the broken finger or toe and wrap it with cloth or tape. If you don't have a splint or cardboard, wrap the injured finger or toe against the finger or toe next to it to immobilize it.
- **Arm**. Carefully place the victim's lower arm at a right angle over her chest. If a bone is broken but does not pierce the skin, wrap the injured area with a magazine or some newspapers padded with a towel or cloth. Tie the magazines above and below the fracture to immobilize

the bone. Put the arm in a sling made with a large piece of cloth or a shirt, and tie it around victim's neck.

- **Leg or hip**. Use two boards padded with towels, or other stiff objects, such as splints. Place boards on either side of the victim's leg and tie them above and below the fracture. If you cannot find splint material, place a rolled-up blanket, pillows, or other padding between victims' legs and tie the legs together to immobilize the injured leg.
- **Upper leg or hip**. Use a splint extending from the victim's arm pit to his foot, and another splint extending from inside the groin to the foot. Tie the splints together and tie the long splint against victim's chest and stomach.
- Call 911.

Burns (redness, swelling, blisters, charring)

- **Minor burns**. Run cool water over the burn for a few minutes until the pain decreases. Put antiseptic/pain-relieving ointment on the burn and bandage if needed.
- **Severe burns**. Immediately remove the victim from source of the fire. If victim's clothes are on fire, quickly throw him to the ground, then smother the flames with a coat, blanket, or whatever is available. If nothing is

available, have him roll around on the ground to smother the fire.

- Carefully remove his clothing and jewelry from the burned area. (Do not remove clothing or jewelry that sticks to the burn.)
- Immerse the burned area in cool (not cold) water for 10 minutes, or apply towels or cloths soaked in cool water. If the burn area is larger than the victim's chest, do not apply water or cover burn.
- Keep burned fingers or toes separated with a clean cloth or non-stick gauze pad.
- Blot the skin dry, lightly bandage the burned area with cloth or gauze pad, then elevate it above the heart. Do not clean the bum area or apply ointment to a severe burn.
- Seek immediate medical help if the victim has trouble breathing, or if his skin is charred, white, or numb.

Carbon Monoxide Poisoning and Smoke Inhalation (breathing problems, loss of consciousness)

- Immediately move the victim into fresh air and have her remain still.
- Call, or have someone else call 911 or the poison control center for instructions.

- If the victim is not breathing or has no pulse, begin CPR (see CPR below).

Chemical Burns (redness, swelling, blisters)

- Check for breathing and pulse and give CPR if needed (see CPR below).
- Remove contaminated clothes and flush the burned area for 10 minutes with cool (not cold) water.
- Blot the skin dry and apply a non-stick dressing.
- Seek medical help in severe burn cases. Choking (coughing, bluish skin color, inability to breathe)

Choking (coughing, bluish skin color, inability to breathe)

- Have the victim cough forcibly to the clear the airway.
- If the victim cannot cough, speak, or breathe, call for medical help.
- Begin Heimlich Maneuver (see Heimlich Maneuver below).

Cold Exposure (uncontrollable shaking, loss of consciousness)

- Check the victim's breathing and pulse and give CPR if needed (see CPR).
- Move victim into warm room near a source of heat.
- Remove cold or wet clothing. Slowly warm victim by having her take a warm (not hot) shower, or by dressing her in warm clothing or blankets. Provide hot liquids (no alcohol) to drink.

CPR (Cardiopulmonary Resuscitation)

- Call 911 or have someone else call.
- Check your surroundings to make sure you're not in danger.
- Shake the victim and ask if she's okay.
- Lay the victim carefully on her back, kneel beside her chest, and tilt her head back slightly by lifting her chin.
- Open her mouth and check for any obstructions such as vomit or food, and remove it if it is loose
- Put your ear to victim's mouth to listen for breathing.
- If the victim is not breathing, pinch her nose shut, seal her mouth with yours, then give 2 slow, full breaths (allow her chest to fall before giving a second breath).

- If the victim's chest does not rise, tilt her head farther back and try again. If her chest still does not rise, use the Heimlich maneuver to clear her airway (see Heimlich Maneuver below)

- After two breaths, check for a pulse by placing your index (first finger) and middle fingers on their wrist, at the base of their thumb. If a pulse is present, continue breathing into the victim until she revives or medical help arrives.

- Adults and large children: 1 breath every 5 seconds.

- Small children and babies: 1 breath every 3 seconds.

- If victim has no pulse, start chest compressions.

- Draw an imaginary line from the victim's armpit to the center of her chest, place one hand on that spot and place the palm of your other hand on top of that hand interlacing your fingers. With your shoulders directly above your hands and your arms straight, press down forcefully.

- **Adults**: Depress victim's breastbone 2 inches. Continue compressions at the rate of "One and two and…" Pause to give two breaths of air after every fifteen chest compressions. Do this four times then check for pulse.

- **Children**: Depress the breastbone 1 1/2 inches using the heel of only one hand. Continue compressions at the rate of "one, two, three..." Pause to give one breath every five compressions. Do this ten times then check for pulse.

- **Babies**: Depress the breastbone 1/2 to 3/4 of an inch by applying moderate pressure with fingertips. Continue compressions at the rate of "one, two, three." Pause to give one breath every five compressions.
- Continue until the victim revives or medical help arrives.

Cuts and Scrapes (bleeding, swelling, pain)

- For severe cuts and lacerations, elevate the wound and apply pressure to stop the bleeding (see Bleeding above).
- For minor cuts and scrapes, clean the wound with soap and water or an antiseptic wipe.
- If the edges of the cut gape open, close it with butterfly bandages or medical tape.
- Coat the wound with small amount of antiseptic/pain-relieving ointment to prevent infection and relieve pain.
- Bandage the wound to keep out dirt and germs.
- Call 911 if the victim has a deep puncture wound or if the wound becomes inflamed or contains pus.

Drowning (unconsciousness, breathing stopped)

- Call 911 or have someone else call.

- Immediately begin CPR (see CPR above). Do not waste time trying to clear water from the victim's lungs.

- If you're a good swimmer and the victim is in shallow water, give CPR and walk her out of the water, or have someone help you walk her out. If you're not a good swimmer, quickly remove her from water and begin CPR immediately.

- Continue CPR until the victim revives or medical help arrives.

- When the victim revives, remove her wet clothing and cover her or dress her to keep her warm.

Ear Problems (pain, dizziness, bleeding)

- **Earache**. Relieve the pain with either hot or cold packs (whichever works best for the victim). Seek medical help if victim experiences dizziness, nausea, fever, discharge, or bleeding.

- **Foreign objects**. Tilt the victim's head so his ear faces ground and shake the object out. If this does not work, take the object out carefully with tweezers. If there is a live insect in the ear, pour a little vinegar or oil into it to kill the insect, then flush it out with warm water.

- **Blood or fluid in the ear**. Lay the victim on his back and cover his ear with a bandage. Seek immediate medical attention.

Electric Shock (unconsciousness, breathing stopped)

- Turn off the electric current, or remove the victim from the source of the current with a nonmetallic object (broom handle, chair, board, etc.).
- Call 911 or have someone else call.
- Check for breathing and pulse, and give CPR if necessary (see CPR above).
- When the victim revives, treat for burns and other injuries.

Eye Problems (pain, objects in eye)

- **Foreign objects**. Have the victim sit in a bright light. Pull her lower eyelid down and have her look up to the right, then to the left, as you look for the object. Remove the object with the corner of a tissue or clean cloth. If you see nothing, pull the upper eyelid down over lower eyelid and let it slide back to dislodge the object. If the object is still in her eye, fold the upper eyelid up over a match stick or cotton swab to view underneath the eyelid. If you cannot see or remove the object, slowly pour a glass of lukewarm water over the eyeball to flush it out. If the victim experiences pain, vision difficulties, or if the object is imbedded in her eyeball, have the victim cover her eye with a soft cloth or bandage and seek immediate medical attention.

- **Chemicals**. Immediately hold the victim's head under lukewarm running water for 15 minutes, or use a glass to pour water over her eyeball. Have the victim pull her eyelid away from her eye so the inside of her eyelid can be washed. Cover her eye with a bandage and seek medical attention.

Fainting (unconsciousness, face pale)

- Have the victim lie down and elevate his feet above his head.
- When the fainting has passed, have him rise slowly to prevent further fainting.
- Call 911 if the fainting does not pass.

Fever (high temperature, warm forehead)

- Have the victim lie down and take her temperature.
- Seek medical help if the fever is over 102º F.
- Give her plenty of fluids and aspirin, or a non-aspirin pain reliever, to relieve the pain and reduce fever.

Frostbite (white or greyish skin, pain)

- Slowly warm frostbitten areas by immersing them in warm (not hot) water, or by wrapping them in warm clothing or blankets. Keep the affected areas covered to keep them warm.
- Do not rub the affected area or apply direct heat (hot pad, hair dryer).
- Seek medical help in cases of severe frostbite to prevent gangrene and loss of fingers or toes.

Head, Neck, and Back Injuries (pain, bleeding, unconsciousness, loss of movement)

- Call 911.
- Do not move victim unless her life is in danger.
- If victim must be moved, immobilize her head between your arms, grab her shirt or jacket at the shoulders and drag her backward. If a blanket is available, carefully roll

the victim onto her side, slide a half-rolled blanket under her back, then carefully roll her onto her back and unroll the blanket. Pull the victim to safety, dragging her head first without bending her back or neck.

- Check for breathing and a pulse and give CPR if necessary (see CPR see above).

Heart Attack (severe chest pain, nausea, dizziness, unconsciousness)

- Call 911 or have someone else call.
- If the victim is conscious have him sit down, loosen his clothing, and give him an aspirin if available.
- If the victim is unconscious, immediately begin CPR (see CPR above).
- When the victim revives, keep him calm and cover him to keep him warm. Do not give him anything to eat or drink.

Heat Exhaustion/heatstroke (faintness, weakness, confusion)

- Have the victim lie down in a cool, shaded area, and elevate her feet.
- Remove her clothing and place cool wet cloths on her forehead and body, or sponge her with cold water. Use a

fan, or fan her with cardboard or a magazine to cool her down.

- Give the victim water to drink. Add 1 teaspoon of salt to 1 quart of water.
- Call 911 if the victim acts confused or her condition does not improve.

Heimlich Maneuver

- Stand behind the victim and place your arms around her waist. Make a fist with one hand and grab it with the other. Place your fist just above the navel, and use a quick forceful thrust, in and up, to expel foreign matter from airway. (If the victim is obese or pregnant, put your fist in middle of victim's breastbone).
- Continue abdominal thrusts until the victim is revived or until help arrives.
- If the victim becomes unconscious, lay her on her back, clear her mouth by sweeping it with your fingers, and gently tilt back her head. Pinch her nose shut, seal your lips around hers, and give her two slow, full breaths. If the victim's chest does not rise, tilt her head back farther to clear her tongue and give her two more breaths.
- If the victim's chest still does not rise, place the heel of your hand on the victim's abdomen just above the navel,

put your other hand on top, then give her five quick forceful thrusts to dislodge object.

- Sweep victim's mouth, and give her two breaths. If her chest does not rise, repeat thrusting, sweeping, and breathing until object is expelled or medical help arrives.

- If the object is expelled but victim stops breathing, begin CPR (see CPR).

- **Self-help**. If you are the one choking and there's no one to help you, place your fist just above your navel, grab it with your other hand, and give yourself quick forceful thrusts, in and up, keeping your elbows out from your body. You can use the edge of a firm object such as a chair or table top to help thrust your fist into your abdomen.

- **Babies and small children**. Sit down and hold the child face down on your knee with your hand supporting his head. Hit him between the shoulder blades four times with the heel of you hand.

- If object is not expelled, turn the child over onto his back and lower his head. Place your fingers on his breastbone just below the nipples, and give him four downward thrusts. Repeat back blows and chest thrusts until the airway is cleared or the baby becomes unconscious.

- If the baby loses consciousness, sweep his mouth with your little finger, and tilt his head back while lifting his jaw. Seal your mouth around his and give him two slow, shallow breaths. If his chest does not rise, tilt his head farther back to clear his tongue and give two more breaths.
- If his chest still does not rise, continue giving him four back blows, four chest thrusts, mouth sweeps, and two breaths until the object is expelled or until medical help arrives.

Insect Bites and Stings (pain, redness, swelling)

- **Bees, hornets, and wasps**. Only honey bees leave a stinger in skin. Remove it by scraping it with a fingernail or knife (do not use tweezers or you may squeeze more venom into your body).
- For multiple stings, soak the affected area in a bath of cool water with baking soda mixed in (1 tablespoon of baking soda to 1 quart of water).
- Clean the affected area with soap and water.
- Call 911 if the victim suffers an allergic reaction (breathing difficulty, loss of consciousness).
- If the victim is not breathing or has no pulse, begin CPR (see CPR above).

- **Spiders and scorpions**. Spider and scorpion bites are rarely fatal, but can be serious for infants and elderly people. If you experience extreme pain from a spider or scorpion bite, put a cold cloth or ice on the bite and seek medical aid. If possible, take the dead spider or scorpion with you for identification.

Nose Problems (bleeding, foreign objects)

- **Nosebleed**. Have the victim sit, then squeeze her nostrils firmly together for 10 minutes so blood can clot. If bleeding persists, pack the nostril with a tissue or a clean cloth. Remove the tissue or cloth after one hour and apply a cool wet cloth over the nose. Seek medical help if bleeding does not stop.
- **Foreign objects**. Have the victim close off the unaffected nostril and blow out object. If the object remains, have her sniff some pepper to sneeze it out. If the object still remains, seek medical help.

Penetration (objects protruding from the body, bleeding, loss of consciousness)

- Do not remove a large object protruding from body. Immobilize it with tape, a gauze bandage, or a belt. If the tape is too tight, loosen it and reapply.
- If the victim is impaled on an immovable object, cut it off if possible and immobilize the part of the object remaining in the body.
- Check for breathing and pulse and give CPR if necessary (see CPR above).
- Treat for shock (see Shock below),
- Call 911.

Poisoning (nausea, vomiting, stomach pain)

- Call your local poison control center (usually listed on the inside cover of your phone book and online), or call your doctor or local hospital for instructions.
- Begin CPR if the victim has no pulse or is not breathing (see CPR above).
- If you cannot reach medical help, stick your finger down the victim's throat to induce vomiting if the poison is known and is not a petroleum product (gasoline, paint

thinner, lighter fluid), or a corrosive substance (drain cleaner, lye, cleaning fluid).

Seizures (twitching movements, drooling, unconsciousness)

- Lay the victim on his side. Remove the victim's glasses and move harmful objects or furniture away from him. Do not restrain him or force anything into his mouth.
- Check for breathing and a pulse after the seizure and give CPR if necessary (see CPR above).
- Loosen his clothing and cover him to keep him warm.
- Seek medical help if this is the victim's first seizure.

Shock (faintness, clammy skin, rapid pulse, rapid breathing, unconsciousness)

- Check for breathing and a pulse and give CPR if necessary (see CPR above).
- Treat the cause of the shock (bleeding, head wound, etc.).
- Keep the victim warm and lying down. Elevate her feet one foot off the ground if her neck and back are uninjured.
- Call 911.

Snakebite (pain, swelling, rapid pulse, paralysis)

- Try to identify the snake then move the victim beyond the striking distance of the snake.
- Make sure the victim remains calm and still to keep the venom from spreading.
- Remove any jewelry from the bite area, remove the shoe if a foot or leg was bitten, and cover the bite area with a sterile bandage.
- DO NOT cut into the wound to try to suck out the venom or apply a tourniquet, ice or water.
- DO NOT give the victim alcohol, caffeinated drinks, or medications.
- Call 911.

Splinters (pain, swelling)

- Use tweezers to remove the object, clean the wound, then cover it with a bandage if necessary.
- If you cannot remove the splinter with tweezers, slit the skin at the end of the splinter with a flame-sterilized needle. Pry up the end of the splinter, then pull it out with tweezers or a fingernail.
- Clean the area with soap and water and bandage it if needed.

Sprains and Strains (swelling, tenderness, movement painful)

- Apply ice or a cool wet cloth to affected joint.
- For sprained ankle or knee, remove the shoe and elevate the leg.
- Wrap the joint with strips of cloth or an ace bandage to immobilize it.

Sunburn (redness, swelling, blisters)

- Cool the victim by immersing her in cool water, or by applying wet cloths to the burn area.
- Have the victim drink fluids.
- Seek medical help or call 911 if the victim is severely burned.

Sunstroke (high temperature, hot skin, rapid pulse, unconsciousness)

- Move the victim out of sun.
- Place the victim in tub of cool (not cold) water and continually pour water over his body to reduce his body temperature. If no tub is available use a spray bottle to spray victim's body, or sponge water over him.

- Call 911 if he has a high temperature, is delirious, or unconscious.

Toothache (pain, swelling, fever)

- To relieve the pain, give the victim aspirin, ibuprofen, or acetaminophen, then dab a small amount of benzocaine or clove oil into the cavity and on the gum area around affected tooth.
- If you have a tooth repair kit, use it to temporarily fill the cavity or broken tooth, or to cement the cap or crown in place until dentist can be seen.

Unconsciousness (victim unmoving and unresponsive)

- Call 911.
- Do not move the victim.
- Check for breathing and a pulse and give CPR if needed (see CPR above).
- Check for a medical tag for a possible cause.
- After the victim recovers, loosen tight clothing, and cover her with a coat or blanket to keep her warm.

FIRST AID KIT

If you don't already have a medical kit, you can buy one at a discount store, drugstore, or online for around $25. This is a very basic kit with first-aid instructions and carrying case. For a few dollars more you can add extra bandages and medications to make a complete kit. The money you spend on a kit that can save your life, or the life of a loved one, could be the best investment you'll ever make.

I've carried versions of the following first-aid kit from Alaska to the Caribbean. I've used it to patch ax and wounds, treat a poison victim, treat a woman with first and second-degree burns, and treat myself for a variety of ailments over the years.

Grace and I have two kits—one we keep in the car under the driver's seat, and one we keep at home under our bathroom sink.

Dressings

- Adhesive bandages (assorted sizes) - to cover small cuts, scrapes, and burns.
- Adhesive tape (1/2-inch roll) to hold gauze pads and bandages in place.
- Butterfly closures (10 medium, 10 large) - to close open wounds.
- Elastic bandage (2-inch roll - to wrap sprains, to apply pressure to bleeding wounds, and for wrapping splints.
- Gauze bandages (2, 2 inch and 1, 3-inch roll) - to wrap large wounds and burns.
- Gauze pads (5, 2" and 5, 4" non-stick pads - to cover large wounds and burns and to use as a compress to stop bleeding.
- Triangular bandage - to use as an arm sling and for bandaging head wounds and large wounds.

Implements

- Needle - to pry out splinters.

- Scissors - to cut bandages and cut clothing away from wounds.
- Thermometer - to take a temperature.
- Tweezers - to remove splinters and foreign objects.

Medications

- Antacid - to relieve heartburn and upset stomach.
- Antibiotic/pain-relieving ointment - to prevent infections and relieve pain in minor cuts, abrasions, and burns.
- Anti-diarrhea medication - to relieve severe diarrhea.
- Antihistamine - to lessen allergic reactions to poisonous plants and insect stings.
- Antiseptic wipes - to clean small wounds.
- Ibuprofen - to relieve pain and reduce fever.
- Oragel - to relieve toothache pain.
- Hydrocortisone cream - to relieve itching due to insect stings, poisonous plants, chemicals, and   conditions.
- Laxative - to temporarily relieve prolonged constipation.

Miscellaneous

- Finger splint - to immobilize sprained or broken finger.
- First-aid pages from this book printed out - to diagnose and treat medical problems.

- Latex gloves - to protect against communicable diseases.
- Moleskin - to cover blisters.
- Safety pins to secure gauze and triangular bandages.
- Tooth repair kit - to temporarily replace fillings and cement loose crowns.

HEALTH CARE TIPS

Medical and Dental Appointments

If you have any medical or dental problems, take care of them now. Schedule any medical exams, dental work, or surgeries now.

If you are pregnant check with your doctor to see what problems might arise if you can't get to a hospital, and find out what provisions can be made to deal with them.

Continuous Care

If you have a medical condition that requires continuous care, talk with your doctor to find out what you can do if you can't get to see him.

Medical Devices

If you are dependent on a medical device, contact the manufacturer to see what you can do if the device were to fail. And if it's an electronic device, and you can afford it, purchase a gasoline generator or solar generator kit to power it.

Medications

If you use prescription medications, keep at least a 2 to 4-week supply in case there are disruptions in drug manufacturing or distribution. If you can afford it, and your doctor will okay it, a 3-month supply would be better.

RECOMMENDED RESOURCES

Visit **www.frugalsurvivalist.com** for information about the products listed below or to purchase them:

First aid book
First aid kit
Thermometer
Tooth repair kit

A BASIC FIRST AID KIT

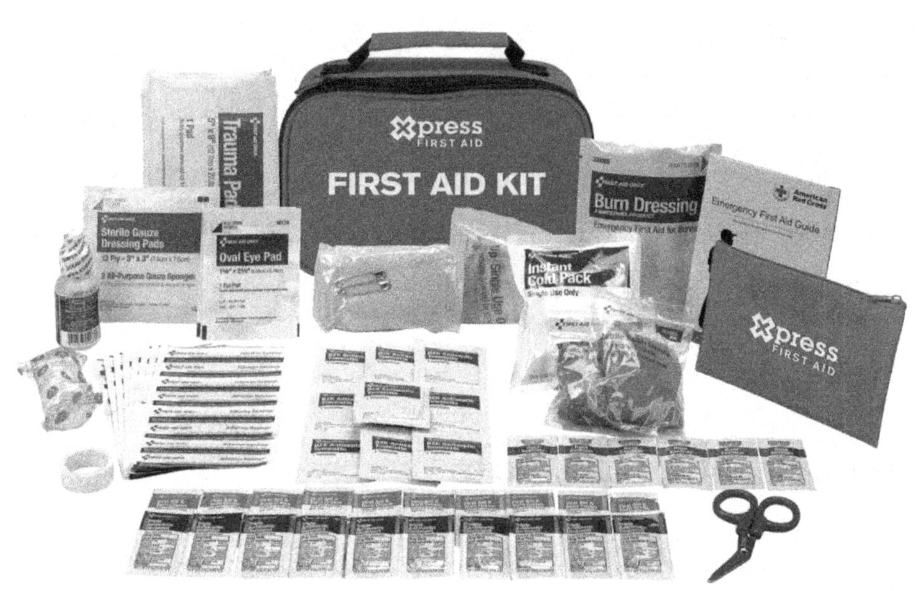

Cold Pack, 4" x 5", 1 Conforming Gauze Roll, 2", 1 CPR Face Shield, 1 Eyewash, 1oz, 1 First Aid Guide, 1 First Aid Tape, 1/2" x 5yd, 1 First Aid/Burn Cream Packets, 0. 9g, 10 Hand Sanitizer Packets, 0. 9g, 6 Nitrile Exam Gloves, 4 Scissors, 1 Sterile Eye Pads, 2 Sterile Gauze Pads, 3" x 3", 4 Trauma Pads, 5" x 9", 2 Triangular Bandage, 40" x 40" x 56", 1 Triple Antibiotic Ointment Packets, 0.5g, 10

- 6 -

FINANCES

"Those who cannot remember the past are condemned to repeat it."
- George Santayana

I'm amazed at how few people realize that markets, all markets, follow cycles. Just look at a line graph of the stock market for the last 100 years and you'll see what looks like a series of mountains and valleys. The line goes up and the line goes down. Every bull market is inevitably followed by a bear market.

The Great Depression

In the months leading up to the Great Depression of 1929 the economy was booming. Businesses were reaping profits at record levels, Banks were extending credit to record numbers of people, and the stock market was hitting record highs.

Charles Schwab, the chairman of Bethlehem Steel, stated: "Never before has American business been as entrenched for prosperity as it has today." Irving Fisher, the foremost economist of his time, declared: "I expect to see the stock market a good deal higher than it is today within a few months."

Even the president of the United States, Herbert Hoover, proclaimed the economy was in the best shape it had been in years.

Then, on October 29, 1929, the stock market crashed. In the span of a few hours millions of investors lost their entire life savings. In the months following the crash millions of people lost their jobs and had to wait in soup lines to get a meal or sell apples and pencils on the street to support their families.

The Great Depression was underway.

The United States stock exchange has crashed 24 times since our country's founding. The economy has experienced a major recession 13 times since the Great Depression ended in 1933, three of which came close to being a financial depression.

Imagine going to your bank as the financial crisis worsens only to find the door locked and a sign that reads "Due to computer problems we will be closed for the day."

"No problem," you tell yourself as you head for the ATM. But as you put your card into the slot for the fourth time and the ATM once again rejects it, you begin to get a little angry.

"Fine," you say to yourself, "I'll just use my credit card." You proceed to drive to your local supermarket to buy groceries and get some cash with your VISA card, but the checker won't take your card because the credit card computers are down.

Now you begin to worry. But you have enough food to tide you over for a few days, so you drive home to try and enjoy the rest of your weekend.

The next day you arrive at your bank bright and early only to find hundreds of angry customers waiting to get in. As the doors open, the crowd rushes to the teller windows and everyone begins withdrawing money. Thinking this is just a temporary problem, you take out just enough money for groceries and incidentals.

The next day you turn on the 6 o'clock news, and your local news anchor is talking about bank closings in your state, and your bank is one of them.

I'm not suggesting runs and bank closings will happen. I'm saying they could happen. And if you don't have any money in reserve you could be left out in the cold, literally.

Now imagine it's mid-December. As you shop for Christmas presents at your local Shop Mart, you notice out of the corner of your eye a special news bulletin on one of the display televisions. The announcer is proclaiming the Dow Jones Industrial's has dropped 3,000 points and is continuing to decline.

You're anxious to call your broker to find out what's happening, so you call him on your cell phone. You dial your stockbroker's number but all you get is a busy signal. You keep trying but to no avail and all the while your stocks are plunging downward.

In 1987, I was working as a financial consultant in Ocala, Florida. In October of that year the stock market crashed. US investors ended up losing more than $1 trillion, and investors worldwide lost more than $4 trillion.

A stock market collapse was averted by some behind-the-scenes wheeling and dealing, and faith in the market was eventually restored. But as an insider, I know we came within a hair's breadth of experiencing the Great Depression of 1929.

In 2008, The Great Recession was a global economic crisis that devastated world financial and real estate markets. It led to major increases in home mortgage foreclosures, and caused millions of people to lose their life savings, their homes, and their jobs.

Once again, we came within a hair's breadth of experiencing a major depression.

Whatever goes up, must inevitably come down. And the higher the market goes, the farther it will fall.

 Right now we're on the verge of a financial crash, some call it "the Greater Depression," the likes of which we've never seen before.

For a complete explanation of why we have financial crashes and why this one may be the worst ever, watch Hidden Secrets Of Money Episode 7 on Youtube.

FINANCIAL SURVIVAL

Here are some things I recommend you do to help you through the hard times ahead:

Acquire cash

After you've stocked up on food, water, survival equipment, and medical supplies, the next thing you need to do is to accumulate cash.

In the beginning stages of a financial meltdown cash is king. You're going to need it if you lose your job and need time to start looking for another one, if your bank starts to limit your withdrawals, or if your bank goes broke. Yes, the money you have in the bank is insured by the FDIC, but it may take a while to get it.

To make sure you have enough money to live on, keep at least one month's worth of living expenses in cash, in a small, portable fireproof safe, hidden in your home. If you can afford it, I recommend having three to six months' worth of cash on hand. Don't keep it in a safety deposit box because if your bank closes you'd be out of luck.

To get some cash you can start by selling things you don't need in a garage sale, on Craig's List, or on eBay. I'll never forget the first garage sale Grace and I had after we got married. We spent $10 on an ad in our local newspaper and, to our surprise, made more than $2,000. And the thing that amazed us was the things that sold first were things we thought were junk.

Consider getting a part time job until you have a cash reserve to see you through the hard times. When I lost my job a few years back, I started a cleaning business to make ends meet. I'm not a big fan of cleaning houses, but it got me through the hard times until my Internet business took off.

Purchase precious metals.

Once you have at least a month's worth of cash, economists who know what they're talking about and have foreseen this coming economic crash, recommend acquiring silver and/or gold coins.

When times get tough, people traditionally turn to precious metals like gold and silver to preserve their capital. In times of economic uncertainty, when stocks and other financial investments start heading south, gold and silver increase in value.

During the inflationary '70's, gold went from $125 to over $800 an ounce. The price of silver increased 1,000% in the same time period. In the just the last 12 months gold has increased 29%, and silver has increased 24%, while the stock market continues to bobble up and down and heads toward a meltdown.

The economists I know recommend buying American Silver Eagle coins, and Gold Eagles if you can afford them. Coins are easier to liquidate than bullion because they are recognizable and because they come in smaller sizes. They are also easy to store, and easy to transport.

American Eagles can be purchased at your local coin dealer or online at companies like JM Bullion, and Kitco.

Cut your expenses

Create a budget by entering all your monthly expenses on a spread sheet, or on a free online budgeting app if you're not familiar with spreadsheets. When you've entered every last thing you spend your money on in a month, start looking for ways to cut your budget to the bone.

Do you need those 550 cable channels you never watch or can you live with basic cable? Can you reduce your insurance premiums by getting a higher deductible? Do you really need those $4 lattes every day or could you make your own for 35 cents? Do you need to eat out when you have cheaper and more nutritious food at home? How much less would your mortgage be if you refinanced your home?

As Ben Franklin once wrote, "A penny saved is a penny earned."

Pay off your credit cards

Pay off your credit cards if it is not a large amount. If it is large, don't pay it off with your savings because you may need that savings in the hard times to come.

The interest you have to pay on your credit card is based on a compounded rate, meaning you're not only paying interest on the amount you spend, but also on the interest accrued. So, for instance, if you have A $1,000 credit card debt and you make payments of $25 a month, you'll end up paying $2,055 to pay it off. That's more than twice what you originally charged!

Do it yourself

During the Great Depression, people made do with what they had, and if they didn't have the money to buy something they needed, they bartered for it or made it themselves.

Instead of paying someone to fix their plumbing, fix their car, or repair house hold items, they did it themselves. There are thousands of tutorials on the Internet that can show you how to fix and do anything under the sun.

I save $450 a year by spending 15 minutes every three months to do my own pest control, $144 a year cutting my own hair, and hundreds more doing my own plumbing and house repairs. Thank you Youtube!

Don't eat out

When I was a financial consultant, I used what I called the pizza principle to demonstrate to clients how much they could save by cutting back on little things like eating out.

One of my clients used to spend $65 a week taking his family out for pizza. I showed him how buying a family-sized pizza at Costco for $10, and a 2-liter bottle of Coke for $1.50, would save him $53 a week, or $2,782 a year. It's the little things that can really make a difference.

Generate a second income

As I mentioned before, when I lost my job as a financial consultant I started a house cleaning business. I'd never cleaned houses before, so I got a book on house cleaning, set up a business checking account, and went to work. It wasn't one of my favorite things to do, but it put food on the table.

During the Great Depression many people did odd jobs or had part time jobs to make ends meet. Think of things you're handy with like carpentry, sewing, plumbing, baking, writing, house cleaning, painting, auto repair, etc.

Call businesses like the one you want to start and ask how much they charge, or go online and Google "how much do (business type, ex: plumbers, house cleaners) make." Once you know how much similar businesses charge, set your price at a little less than theirs, and run an ad in your local newspaper, or Craig's list.

If you're not handy with anything you can go online to view tutorials on how to do virtually anything.

Think about moving

During the Great Depression a series of droughts and dust storms caused thousands of farms to go under in the Southern Plains region of the US. The area, known as the Dust Bowl, saw the largest migration in US history, with millions of people abandoning their homes and farms, and moving to places like California where they could find work.

With unemployment rising to levels that we haven't seen since the Great Depression, many Americans are going online to find jobs outside of their communities.

Sites like Google For Jobs, a search engine that compiles job listings from a number of sources, and Indeed, a job website that lists jobs from thousands of websites and newspapers, are a great way to search for out-of-area jobs, and even in-area jobs.

Get connected

During the Great Depression people banded together to help each other through the hard times, whether it was feeding a starving family, giving them some clothes, or providing a place to sleep. Those who had more gave whatever they could spare to those who had less.

Get to know your neighbors, for they may be able to help your through the coming crisis, or you may be able to help them. Get familiar with your local charities, church groups, and food banks for the same reasons, and support them if you can.

Remember: "This too, will pass."

We've gone through numerous recessions, depressions, wars, and civil unrest, and we've always come through them with flying colors. Years after the Great Depression ended, our country experienced a wave of unprecedented prosperity and a greater sense of community and wellbeing.

We did it before, and we'll do it again.

RECOMMENDED RESOURCES

Visit **www.frugalsurvivalist.com** for information about the products listed below or to purchase them:

Fireproof safes

Gold and silver coin dealer

FIREPROOF SAFE

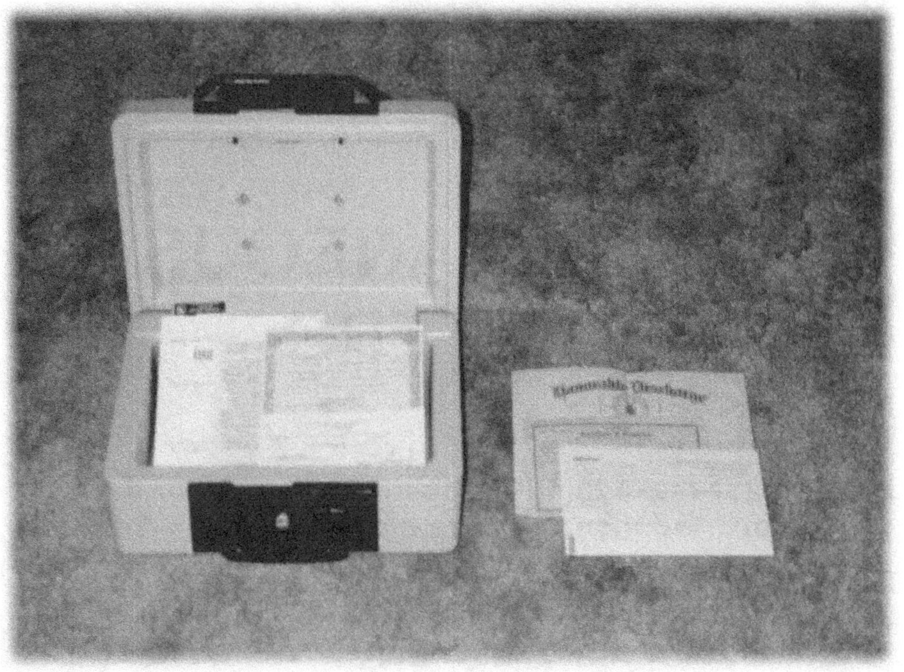

Portable fireproof safe.

- 7 -

MISCELLANEOUS MATTERS

"Some people make things happen. Some wait for things to happen. And then there are those who say, "What happened?"

- Unknown

HOME SECURITY

If phone systems went down and you had no way to contact your local police, you'd be totally dependent on yourself for protection from an assault or robbery.

A few simple, inexpensive precautions can mean the difference between a criminal entering your home, and a criminal walking away because he couldn't enter your home.

When it comes to home security, simple is best.

Make sure you have dead bolt locks on your doors and remember to keep them locked, even during the daytime. A peephole installed in your door makes it easy to identify people. Don't let anyone in your house you can't identify.

If you don't know who's at your door, keep it shut and have them show you their identification by holding it up to your peephole. Then, if you're still unsure about the person, call their company or station to verify their credentials.

If you have electronic locks, make sure you have a manual override in case of power outages.

Make sure you secure your windows and sliding-glass doors. A small hole drilled through the window frame and window track, with a small nail inserted to secure them, is a simple way prevent windows and sliding glass doors from being opened.

Install a lock on your garage door if it doesn't have one. Garages are becoming a favorite means of entry among thieves because garage doors are so easy to open with a programmable remote control, or with a crowbar.

Clear all shrubbery and prune all trees near your windows and doors (burglars can hide behind them).

A neat trick I read about in a burglary prevention book is to put a "Beware of Dog" sign on your front door, and a large dog bowl next to the door. When 50 professional burglars were interviewed for the book, 9 out of 10 said they would pass on a house they thought had a dog inside.

If you have an electronic security system, make sure it has backup batteries in case the electricity goes out.

To make sure your home is secure, do what Grace and I did. Lock yourself out of your home and see if you can get in. If you can't get in, odds are neither can a burglar. Most burglars are in search of an easy entry and will avoid a well-secured, well-lit home.

Weapons

Gun ownership is a personal choice.

A number of people are stockpiling weapons and preparing for a world-wide catastrophe resembling a *Road Warrior* movie.

Assuming there will be absolutely no food anywhere, and that civilized people will turn into crazed animals, they may be right. History, however, tells a different story.

During times of catastrophes people have more of a tendency to pull together than to commit acts of violence. During the Great Depression there were few crimes committed because people were destitute. People who had food and shelter extended their homes and their hearts to those who didn't.

Things have changed since, but people are pretty much the same. I believe a major crisis will bring out the best in us rather than the worst.

Grace and I live in a Beaver Cleaver type of neighborhood in the Arizona countryside. The last major crime spree we had was a few years ago when a couple of drunk teenagers decided to go riding around the neighborhood with a baseball bat and knock over mailboxes.

I seriously doubt we'll have any problems with crime even if the crisis escalates, so Grace and I have not stockpiled weapons and ammunitions in anticipation of marauding gangs pillaging our neighborhood. If someone came knocking on our door in search of food we would help them rather than shoot them.

Based on the number of people who shoot themselves, or whose kids shoot other kids with their guns, most people are safer not owning a gun. Statistically, a gun in your home is 23 times more likely to kill a friend or family member than an intruder. Last year there were 241 unintended shootings by children, resulting in more than 100 deaths.

Your circumstances, however, may be different than ours. If you decide that owning a gun is a good idea, make sure you take a gun safety course. I would also suggest taking a course that teaches you how to handle yourself in survival situations.

TRANSPORTATION

The most likely problems with transportation systems will be due to gas stations going broke, and the disruption of the production and transportation of fuel. Gas shortages will not only affect you, they will also affect airline, train, and bus transportation too.

Public Transportation

Companies the run busses, taxis, Ubers, and Lyfts are all susceptible to bankruptcy, so these services may not be available if things get really rough

Although congress has instituted the stimulus bill that includes $58 billion in aid for airlines, several airlines have already filed for bankruptcy. And it's likely that other airlines, both in the US and abroad, will be forced to do the same.

Cars

If gas stations go broke, gas will be hard to find. If gas supplies are disrupted, gas stations will run out of gas. And if the power goes down, gas pumps won't work. So unless you have a solar-powered car, you may experience some major difficulties getting around.

I recommend keeping your car at least half full in case gas supplies run low or gas pumps go down. I don't recommend storing large amounts of gasoline as it is highly volatile, however storing a couple of five-gallon containers filled with gas might not be a bad idea.

Get your car ready for possible parts shortages by replacing worn hoses, belts, and tires. And check your oil, battery, and fluid levels.

Bicycles

Grace and I have two bicycles. They're easy to use, easy to maintain, and on level terrain we can easily pedal them more than a hundred miles in a day. At less than $200 each, they are an extremely economical form of alternative transportation. If you're on a budget you can buy a good used bike for less than $50.

I've pedaled bicycles through wilderness roads in Alaska, on dirt roads in the Caribbean, and commuting to work in Florida and Arizona. I can't think of a better form of back-up transportation.

If you live in the country and will be traveling on dirt roads, I recommend buying a mountain bike. If you live in a town or city where most roads are paved, get a cross bike or a touring bike. They're faster and require less effort than a mountain bike.

Learning to repair a bicycle is easy once you've done it. YouTube has a bazillion videos on bike repair. A simple tool kit costing less than $50 is all you'll need to keep your bicycle in tip top shape. You might also want to purchase a spare inner tube and a tire repair kit.

To transport light loads I recommend using a seat bag or a small backpack. For heavy loads you can buy a bicycle rack and a pair of panniers (bicycle saddle bags).

Mopeds

Mopeds are a cross between a motorcycle and a bicycle. You can pedal them like a bicycle or ride them like a motorcycle. Most have a top speed of about 20 miles per hour, and will go 150 miles on a gallon of gas. If you were to store just 10 gallons of gas, you could commute 25 miles a day, every day, for 2 months. How's that for cheap transportation.

Boats

If you live near a river, lake, or the ocean, a boat is an ideal way to get around. Even a small boat like a canoe or kayak will carry a lot of cargo, and weather all but the roughest of storms. If storage is a problem, a number of manufacturers make folding kayaks and rowboats.

I've kayaked and canoed all over Alaska, Canada, and Florida. Not only is it a great way to haul supplies, it's also relaxing, and great exercise.

If you buy a canoe or kayak, make sure you take a course or read a book on how to paddle and handle it.

New kayaks and canoes can be purchased for $200 to $2,000. Used, they can be bought for around $75 to $500.

Walking

The secret to covering long distances on foot is to walk at a pace that's comfortable, to use minimum motion, and to keep a steady, even pace. Doing this, you can cover 20 miles a day on level ground if you're in halfway decent shape.

The secret to comfortable walking is having comfortable shoes or boots. Forget the nonsense you hear from salesmen who tell you "You have to break them in." If your shoes aren't comfortable from the moment you put them on, they never will be.

You don't need anything fancy. Just make sure they're comfortable and sturdy.

The last time I bought a pair of walking shoes I drove the salesperson crazy trying on every shoe in the store. Lucidly the salesperson was my wife, Grace, and she understood.

Walking may be your primary means of transportation if things go haywire, so don't be afraid to spend a little extra for good shoes.

COMMUNICATION

Radio

If your electricity goes out, and your cell phone battery is dead, a transistor radio can be a life saver in an emergency situation. They're cheap, they're reliable, and in addition to entertaining you with music, you can tune into your local news station for the latest information about the crisis, and also access the Emergency Alert System.

The Emergency Alert system, or EAS, is a national public warning system used by state and local authorities to deliver important emergency information, such as weather information, imminent threats, AMBER alerts, local incident information targeted to specific areas, and emergency information from the president.

You can purchase a battery powered radio for $10, or a combination hand crank/solar powered radio that will also charge your cell phone for $20.

Cell phone

There is a myth that if the electricity goes out in your area, cell phone towers, which require electricity to broadcast a signal, will go out too, and you won't have service.

Not so. All the major carriers have generators and backup plans so they can maintain service. However, your cell phone may malfunction and leave you without a means of communication.

In that case, it's wise to have an extra cell phone. Cheap, refurbished cell phones can be had for less than $50, and may be a godsend if your $1,000 iPhone goes on the blink.

Walkie Talkie

A set of walkie talkies with a range of 15 miles can be purchased for less than $40. These would be useful if you're out of cell phone range and want to keep track of your family.

Citizen's Band Radio

Years ago, CB radios were all the rage. Now, thanks to the advent of cell phones, they've fallen by the wayside. Hardly anyone uses them anymore, so there aren't a lot of people you can contact for help.

Ham Radio

With a ham radio you can receive and broadcast messages around the globe. You will, however, need a license to operate one and they are expensive. Ham radios can be powered by batteries or solar panels.

ENTERTAINMENT

Electrical blackouts mean no television, radio, stereo, or computer games, unless they're battery operated. This could cause some people to go stark raving nuts. But there are alternative means of entertainment that could prove to be more fun than watching reruns of The Bachelor or Friends, or blasting the Lord of Terror with your joystick for the one-thousandth time.

Books

Read a good book lately? Being an author, I could extol the virtues of books versus television from now until kingdom come. Suffice it to say, books are a wonderful way to exercise your imagination instead of letting your mind go flabby as you sit in front of an electronic box and passively absorb everything it spews out.

An electrical blackout might be just the opportunity you need to learn something you've always wanted to learn, or to read that book you've been wanting to read. Your local library has tens-of-thousands of books you can check out or download online, and the Internet has a number of sites that let you read books for free, like Project Gutenberg, which has more than 60,000 titles available.

A good paperback book can be one of the cheapest investments you'll ever make. In fact, it might even pay dividends. A book I purchased for $5.50, titled *Freedom From Backaches*, saved me from having a $2,500 back operation by showing me how one simple exercise could relieve my backache pain. That book was literally worth its weight in gold.

Indoor Games

Grace and I have had some of the best times of our lives playing games with family and friends. Unlike watching television or videos, playing games with other people brings you closer together because you communicate and get to know each other.

Whether playing bridge with my mom, hearts with my sisters, or Jenga with Grace's son and his family, Grace and I have experienced a whole new world of fun and enjoyment with our family.

If you're on a budget a $6 book, *Hoyle's Rules of Games*, and a $3 deck of cards will give you and your family or friends endless hours of entertainment.

Some of our favorite games include bridge, hearts, *Jenga, Pictionary, Trivial Pursuit, Scrabble, Apples To Apples, Clue, Ben There Done That*, chess, checkers, and the ever-popular spoons, a simple game that never ceases to make everyone laugh themselves silly.

Outdoor Games

If you're more the physical type, there's nothing like a game of volleyball, soccer, softball, touch football, frisbee, catch, tag, or hackey sack to get the old heart pumping and the adrenaline flowing. For the less physical, a game of badminton, croquet, cornhole, lawn darts, bocce ball, or horseshoes, will keep you entertained.

Musical Instruments

Now may be the perfect opportunity to improve your musical skills. If you don't have a musical instrument, it may be time to buy that guitar or flute you've always wanted.

ATTITUDE

For some people, the financial crisis is the figment of a number of people's imaginations. For others, it's something to be dreaded and feared. For still others, it's an adventure, something that will test our patience, our determination, and our survival skills.

If you haven't read or listened to the research on financial meltdowns, you probably don't think anything is going to happen, and all the fuss that's being made is a bunch of nonsense. In that case ignorance is bliss, and I wish you well.

If you've done your research, you know that the crisis is very real, and that problems, whether major or minor, will occur. The problem now is trying to figure out what could happen, and how you can prepare for it.

As I've said, nobody really knows how bad things are going to get. The best you can do is hope for the best and prepare for the worst. The more you prepare for a financial crisis, the more confident you'll feel and the less you'll fear it.

Get your family involved in creating a survival plan. Talk to your kids and parents about what may happen and what you can do. You may be surprised at the help and information they can give you. Put your older children in charge of an area of preparation.

Survival Weekend

When you finish acquiring your survival food, water, and equipment, schedule test run. Turn off the electricity and gas for a day and see how well you do living without them. Light your kerosene lamps, use your battery-operated radio, cook on your stove, play games, and treat it as a camp out.

Next day, evaluate what you did right, what you did wrong, and what extra food or equipment you may want to have.

As Aristotle once wrote: "Happiness belongs to the self-sufficient."

RECOMMENDED RESOURCES

Visit **www.frugalsurvivalist.com** for information about the products listed below or to purchase them:

Security signs

Security alarms

Bicycles and accessories

Radios

Rechargeable batteries

Walkie talkies

Solar battery charger

Indoor and outdoor games

ENTERTAINMENT

Transistor Radio, Stereo, Solar Battery Charger, Rechargeable Batteries, Games Book, Book, Games

- 8 -

DOCUMENTS, RECORDS AND CHECKLISTS

"To error is human. To really screw up takes a computer."
- Unknown

Computers could malfunction or even shut down, and the records stored in them could be lost forever.

The records stored at your bank or brokerage house could be compromised or lost. It could mean problems with ATM systems, or credit and debit cards.

If you work with a computer you know that heart-sinking feeling that happens when it crashes and you lose a file. If that file wasn't saved, it's gone forever.

The same holds true of any documents or records you want to keep - if it's not on paper, on a flash drive, or on an external hard drive, you run the risk of losing it if your computer crashes.

The following is a list of documents and records you should store in a safe place. I recommend storing them on paper or on a flash drive, and keeping them in a portable, fireproof safe in case you have a fire or your need to evacuate your home.

Documents And Records

- Bank statements
- Birth certificates
- Contracts
- Credit card statements
- Deeds
- Household inventory
- Insurance policies
- Immunization records
- Important telephone numbers
- Income tax returns
- Loan payment records
- Marriage certificate
- Receipts (medical, tax, rent, etc.)
- Social Security cards
- Stocks and bonds

- Titles (car, house, boat, etc.)
- Trust documents
- Passports
- Will

In addition to keeping copies of the above items, make sure your doctor and dentist have your medical and dental records on paper or on a backup hard drive.

The following are checklists of emergency preparedness items:

Clothing And Bedding

- Blankets or sleeping bags
- Gloves
- Hats
- Sturdy shoes
- Rain coat
- Thermal underwear
- Winter coat

Entertainment

- Books
- Cards
- CDs
- CD player
- DVDS
- DVD player
- Games (indoor and outdoor)
- Games rule book
- Hobby and craft equipment
- MP3 player

- Musical instruments
- Sports equipment

Health

- Dentures cleaner (extra)
- Contact lenses (extra pair)
- Contact lens cleaner (extra)
- Eyeglasses (extra pair)
- First aid kit
- Personal medical devices
- Personal medications (extra)
- Vitamins (extra)

Heating, Cooling, Cooking, And Lighting

- Heater with fuel
- Fan (battery operated)
- Flashlights with batteries
- Lamps with batteries and/or fuel
- Lighters
- Matches
- Solar battery charger
- Stove and/or solar oven

Hygiene

- Baby wipes (extra)
- Body lotion (extra)
- Clothesline and clothespins
- Diapers (extra)
- Dish pan
- Laundry detergent (extra)
- Feminine supplies (extra)
- Foam cups, plates, and bowls

- Garbage bags
- Hair products (extra)
- Personal grooming items
- Plastic utensils
- Portable toilet
- Soap (extra)
- Shampoo (extra)
- Sunscreen (extra)
- Tooth brushes and toothpaste (extra)
- Toilet paper (extra)
- Wash tub

Food And Water

- Baby food
- Canned food
- Canned juices
- Clorox
- Condiments and spices
- Dehydrated food
- Dried beans
- Freeze-dried food
- Grains
- MREs (Meals Ready to Eat)
- Pet food
- Special-diet food
- Water (treated)
- Water containers
- Water filter

Tools And Supplies

- Can opener
- Crowbar
- Duct tap

- Drill (hand or battery operated)
- Files (wood and metal)
- Glue (wood and all-purpose)
- Hacksaw
- Hammer
- Nails (assorted)
- Plastic sheeting (clear)
- Pliers
- Rake
- Saw
- Screws (assorted)
- Screw driver (standard and Phillips)
- Shovel
- Shut-off wrench (gas, water)
- Tape (clear)
- Tape measure
- Utility knife
- Wrench (adjustable)

Miscellaneous

- Area map
- Cash or traveler's checks
- Extra cell phone
- Fire extinguisher (ABC type)
- Radio
- Sewing kit
- Sunglasses (extra)

RECOMMENDED RESOURCES

Visit **www.frugalsurvivalist.com** for information about the products listed below or to purchase them:

Fireproof safes
Fireproof document bag

DOCUMENTS AND RECORDS

Portable fireproof safe with documents and records.

IN CONCLUSION

"This, too, shall pass."

Rumi

These words from the Persian poet Rumi are as true today as they were more than 800 years ago. Nothing stays the same, and that's especially true of the economy.

A chart of economic cycles looks like a roller coaster – up and down, recession then recovery. So take heart in the fact that the coming depression will turn around at some point and all will be well once again.

And keep in mind …

"If you have food in your refrigerator, clothes on your back, a roof over your head, and a place to sleep, you are richer than 75% of this world.

"If you have money in the bank, in your wallet, and spare change in a dish someplace, you are among the top 8% of the world's wealthy.

"If you hold up your head with a smile on your face and are truly thankful, you are blessed because the majority can, but most do not.

"If you can read this message, you are more blessed that over two billion people in the world who cannot read anything at all.

"You are blessed in so many ways you may never even know.

"So count your blessings and be thankful you are who you are."

- Unknown

If you liked this book, I would like to ask you to do me a favor and leave a review on Amazon. Just go to the page on Amazon where you purchased my book, scroll down to where you see "Review This Product" on the left side, and click "Write A Customer Review."

Thank you!